Les Liaisons Dangereuses

A Play

Christopher Hampton

From the novel by
Choderlos de Laclos

Samuel French—London
New York—Sydney—Toronto—Hollywood

LES LIAISONS DANGEREUSES

First produced by the Royal Shakespeare Company at The Other Place, Stratford-upon-Avon on 24th September, 1985, with the following cast of characters:

La Marquise de Merteuil	Lindsay Duncan
Mme de Volanges	Fiona Shaw
Cécile Volanges	Lesley Manville
Major-domo	Hugh Simon
Le Vicomte de Valmont	Alan Rickman
Azolan	Christopher Wright
Mme de Rosemonde	Margery Mason
La Présidente de Tourvel	Juliet Stevenson
Émilie	Mary Jo Randle
Le Chevalier Danceny	Sean Baker

Various servants in the Merteuil, Rosemonde, Tourvel and Valmont households

The play was directed by Howard Davies
Designed by Bob Crowley
Lighting by Chris Parry. Music by Ilona Sekacz

Subsequently produced at The Pit, Barbican, on 8th January 1986, with the following cast of characters:

La Marquise de Merteuil	Lindsay Duncan
Mme de Volanges	Fiona Shaw
Cécile Volanges	Lesley Manville
Major-domo	Hugh Simon
Le Vicomte de Valmont	Alan Rickman
Azolan	Christopher Wright
Mme de Rosemunde	Margery Mason
La Présidente de Tourvel	Juliet Stevenson
Émilie	Mary Jo Randle
Le Chevalier Danceny	Sean Baker

The play directed by Howard Davies
Designed by Bob Crowley
Lighting by Chris Parry. Music by Ilona Sekacz

The action of the play takes place in various salons and bedrooms in a number of hôtels and châteaux in and around Paris, and in the Bois de Vincennes, one autumn and winter in the 1780s.

ACT I

ACT II

The action of the play takes place during one autumn and winter in the 1780s

Note: Both for practical reasons and to enhance the fluidity of the action, the play was performed without breaks (except for the interval) or set-changes, up to the end of Act II, Scene 7, when the set was cleared, except for a table and three chairs, for the last two scenes.   C.H.

To Roger

ACT I

SCENE 1

A warm evening in August

The principal salon in the Paris hôtel of Mme la Marquise de Merteuil. The Marquise, a respectable widow of considerable means, is playing piquet with her cousin, Mme de Volanges, who is herself a widow. Sitting next to Mme de Volanges, watching her play and politely stifling the occasional yawn, is her daughter Cécile, a slim and attractive blonde girl of fifteen. Suggestions of great opulence. The large playing cards slap down on one another

Merteuil interrupts the game to examine Cécile with some care

Merteuil Well, my dear.

Cécile, who has been daydreaming, starts, not quite sure, for a second, if it's she who's being addressed

So you've left the convent for good?
Cécile Yes, Madame.
Merteuil And how are you adapting to the outside world?
Cécile Very well, I think. I'm so excited to have my own bedroom and dressing room.
Volanges I've advised her to watch and learn and be quiet except when spoken to. She's very naturally still prone to confusion. Yesterday she was under the impression my shoemaker had come for dinner.
Cécile It wasn't that, Maman, it was when he fell to his knees and caught hold of my foot. It startled me.
Merteuil No doubt you thought he was attempting to propose marriage.
Cécile I ... (*She breaks off, blushing*)
Merteuil Never mind, my dear, you'll soon get used to it. We must see what we can devise for your amusement.

The game resumes. Silence.

After a time, Merteuil's Major-domo appears, advances hurriedly across the room and murmurs something in Merteuil's ear

(*Sighing*) Oh, very well, show him up.
The Major-domo bows and withdraws

Merteuil turns back to the others

Valmont is here.
Volanges You receive him, do you?
Merteuil Yes. So do you.

Volanges I thought perhaps that under the circumstances ...
Merteuil Under what circumstances? I don't believe I have any grounds for self-reproach ...
Volanges On the contrary. As far as I know, you're virtually unique in that respect.
Merteuil ... and, of course, if I had, he would no longer be calling on me.

Cécile has been following this exchange closely, frowning in the attempt to make sense of it. Now Mme de Volanges turns to her

Volanges Monsieur le Vicomte de Valmont, my child, whom you very probably don't remember, except that he is conspicuously charming, never opens his mouth without first calculating what damage he can do.
Cécile Then why do you receive him, Maman?
Volanges Everyone receives him. He has a distinguished name, a large fortune and a very pleasant manner. You'll soon find that society is riddled with such inconsistencies: we're all aware of them, we all deplore them and in the end we all accommodate to them. Besides which, people are quite rightly afraid to provoke his malice. No one has the slightest respect for him; but everyone is very nice to him. (*She breaks off*)

The Major-domo reappears, escorting Le Vicomte de Valmont, a strikingly elegant figure. He crosses the room and bows formally to Merteuil in a gesture which takes in the others. The Mayor-domo exits

Valmont Madame.
Merteuil Vicomte.
Volanges What a pleasant surprise.
Valmont How delightful to see you, Madame.
Volanges You remember my daughter, Cécile.
Valmont Well, indeed, but who could have foretold she would flower so gracefully?

Cécile simpers and looks away. Valmont turns back to Merteuil

I wanted to call on you before leaving the city.
Merteuil Oh, I'm not sure we can allow that. Why should you want to leave?
Valmont Paris in August, you know: and it's time I paid a visit to my old aunt, I've neglected her disgracefully.
Merteuil I approve of your aunt. She takes such an intelligent interest in the young, she's been able to maintain a kind of youthfulness of her own. All the same ...
Volanges Will you please give Madame de Rosemonde our warmest regards? She's been good enough to invite us to stay at the château, and I hope perhaps later in the season ...
Valmont I shall make a point of it, Madame. Please don't let me interrupt your game.
Volanges I think I may have lost enough for this evening.

In the ensuing silence, they become aware that Cécile is fast asleep

Valmont Your daughter evidently finds our conversation intriguing.

Valmont laughs and Merteuil joins in, causing Cécile to jerk awake in confusion

Cécile Oh, I'm sorry, I ...
Volanges I think it's time we took you home.
Cécile I'm used to being asleep by nine at the convent.
Valmont So I should hope.

The ladies rise to their feet and Merteuil signals to a Footman, who moves over to escort Mme de Volanges and Cécile from the room, amid general salutations

Valmont bows to them and waits, a little apart. Eventually, Merteuil moves back towards him. They're alone together and look at each other for a while before Merteuil speaks, in a quite different tone

Merteuil Your aunt?
Valmont That's right.
Merteuil Whatever for? I thought she'd already made arrangements to leave you all her money.
Valmont She has. But there are other considerations, family obligations, that kind of thing.
Merteuil Do you know why I summoned you here this evening?
Valmont I'd hoped it might be for the pleasure of my company.
Merteuil I need you; to carry out a heroic enterprise. Something for your memoirs.
Valmont I don't know when I shall ever find the time to write my memoirs.
Merteuil Then I'll write them.

Silence. Valmont smiles at her

You remember when Gercourt left me?
Valmont Yes.
Merteuil And went off with that fat mistress of yours, whose name escapes me?
Valmont Yes, yes.
Merteuil No one has ever done that to me before. Or to you, I imagine.
Valmont I was quite relieved to be rid of her, frankly.
Merteuil No, you weren't.

Silence

One of Gercourt's more crass and boring topics of conversation was what exactly he would look for in a wife, what qualities, when the moment came for him, as he put it, to settle down.
Valmont Yes.
Merteuil He had a ludicrous theory that blondes were inherently more modest and respectable than any other species of girl and he was also unshakeably prejudiced in favour of convent education. And now he's found the ideal candidate.
Valmont Cécile Volanges?

Merteuil Very good.

Valmont And her sixty thousand a year, that must have played some part in his calculations.

Merteuil I tell you, if she were an uncloistered brunette, she could be worth twice that, and he wouldn't go near her. His priority, you see, is a guaranteed virtue.

Valmont I wonder if I'm beginning to guess what it is you're intending to propose.

Merteuil Gercourt is with his regiment in Corsica until October. That should give you plenty of time.

Valmont You mean to ... ?

Merteuil She's a rosebud.

Valmont You think so?

Merteuil And he'd get back from honeymoon to find himself the laughing-stock of Paris.

Valmont Well ...

Merteuil Yes. Love and revenge: two of your favourites.

Silence. Valmont considers for a moment. Finally, he shakes his head, smiling

Valmont No, I can't.

Merteuil What?

Valmont You know how difficult I find it to disobey your orders. But really, I can't.

Merteuil Why not?

Valmont It's too easy. It is. What is she, fifteen, she's seen nothing, she knows nothing, she's bound to be curious, she'd be on her back before you'd unwrapped the first bunch of flowers. Any one of a dozen men could manage it. I have my reputation to think of.

Merteuil I think you underestimate her. She's very pretty, and she has a rather promising air of languor.

Valmont You mean, she falls asleep a lot? Well, perhaps your Belleroche is the man for her.

Merteuil Belleroche is an idealist.

Valmont Oh, bad luck, I knew there was something the matter with him.

Merteuil There is someone who's already fallen for her: young Danceny. He goes round to sing duets with her.

Valmont And you think he'd like to try a little close harmony?

Merteuil Yes, but he's as timid and inexperienced as she is, we couldn't rely on him. So, you see, it'll just have to be you.

Valmont I hate to disappoint you.

Merteuil I think you really are going to refuse me. Aren't you?

Silence. Valmont looks at her

Valmont I can see I'm going to have to tell you everything.

Merteuil Of course you are.

Valmont Yes. Well. My trip to the country to visit my more or less immortal aunt. The fact of the matter is that it's the first step towards the most ambitious plan I've ever undertaken.

Merteuil Well, go on.

Valmont You see, my aunt is not on her own just at the moment. She has a young friend staying with her. Madame de Tourvel.

Merteuil Yes.

Valmont She is my plan.

Merteuil You can't mean it.

Valmont Why not? To seduce a woman famous for strict morals, religious fervour and the happiness of her marriage: what could possibly be more prestigious?

Merteuil I think there's something very degrading about having a husband for a rival. It's humiliating if you fail and commonplace if you succeed. Where is he, anyway?

Valmont He's presiding over some labyrinthine case in Burgundy, which I'm reliably informed will drag on for months.

Merteuil I can't believe this. Apart from anything else, she's such a frump. Bodice up to her ears in case you might catch a glimpse of a square inch of flesh ...

Valmont You're right, clothes don't suit her.

Merteuil How old is she?

Valmont Twenty-two.

Merteuil And she's been married ...?

Valmont Two years.

Merteuil Even if you succeed, you know what?

Valmont What?

Merteuil All you'll get from her is what she gives her husband. I don't think you can hope for any actual pleasure. They never let themselves go, those people. If you ever make her heart beat faster, it won't be love, it'll be fear. I sometimes wonder about you, Vicomte. How could you make such a fool of yourself over a complete nonentity?

Valmont Take care, now, you're speaking of the woman I ...

Merteuil Yes?

Valmont I've set my heart on.

Silence. Valmont smiles at her

I haven't felt so strongly about anything since you and I were together.

Merteuil And you're going to pass up this wonderful opportunity for revenge?

Valmont If I have to.

Merteuil You don't have to. I won't tell anyone about this bizarre aberration of yours.

Valmont I think you'll have to wait at least until I've had her before I can allow you to insult her. And I can't agree with your theory about pleasure. You see, I have no intention of breaking down her prejudices. I want her to believe in God and virtue and the sanctity of marriage, and still not be able to stop herself. I want passion, in other words. Not the kind we're used to, which is as cold as it's superficial, I don't get much pleasure out of that any more. No. I want the excitement of watching her betray everything that's most important to her. Surely you understand that. I thought betrayal was your favourite word.

Merteuil No, no, cruelty, I always think that has a nobler ring to it.

Valmont You're terrible, you're a hundred times worse than I'll ever be; since we started this little mission, you've made many more converts than I have, you make me feel like an amateur.

Merteuil And so you are; really, you might just as well be in love.

Valmont Well, if love is not being able to think of anything else all day or dream of anyone else all night, perhaps I am: that's why I must have her, to rescue myself from this ridiculous position.

Merteuil Love is something you use, not something you fall into, like a quicksand, don't you remember? It's like medicine, you use it as a lubricant to nature.

They look at each other

Valmont How is Belleroche?

Merteuil Well, he *is* in love. I thought it might be time to end it last week, I tried to pick a quarrel, but he looked so woebegone, I relented, and we spent the best night we've ever had. Since then, of course, he's been more assiduous than ever. But I'm keeping him at arm's length because I'm so pleased with him. He hasn't learned that excess is something you reserve for people you're about to leave.

Valmont So you're not about to leave him?

Merteuil No, I told you, at the moment I'm very pleased with him.

Valmont And he's currently your only lover?

Merteuil Yes.

Valmont I think you should take another. I think it most unhealthy, this exclusivity.

Merteuil You're not jealous, are you?

Valmont Well, of course I am. Belleroche is completely undeserving.

Merteuil I thought he was one of your closest friends.

Valmont Exactly, so I know what I'm talking about. No, I think you should organize an infidelity. With me, for example.

Merteuil But we decided it was far more important to preserve our friendship and to be able to trust each other implicitly.

Valmont Are you sure that wasn't just a device to heighten our pleasure?

Merteuil You refuse to grant me a simple favour, and then you expect to be indulged.

Valmont It's only because it is so simple. It wouldn't feel like a conquest. I have to follow my destiny, you see. I have to be true to my profession.

Merteuil Well ...

Long silence. They look at each other, Merteuil amused, Valmont eager

In that case, come back when you've succeeded with Madame de Tourvel.

Valmont Yes?

Merteuil And I will offer you ... a reward.

Valmont My love.

Merteuil But I shall require proof.

Valmont Certainly.
Merteuil Written proof.
Valmont Ah.
Merteuil Not negotiable.

Valmont rises to his feet and bows. Merteuil watches him, smiling

Valmont And I'm sure you'll find someone to help you out with the little Volanges.
Merteuil She's so lovely. If my morals were less austere, I'd take it on myself.
Valmont You are an astonishing woman.
Merteuil Thank you.
Valmont I'm only sorry you haven't sufficient confidence in me to give me my reward in advance.
Merteuil Goodnight, Vicomte.

Valmont kisses her hand, releases it and stands looking at her for a moment, before turning away

SCENE 2

Three weeks later. Early evening. The principal salon in Mme de Rosemonde's château in the country. The late sun slants through the french windows

Valmont is interviewing Azolan, his valet de chambre, *a dapper young man, resplendent in the livery of a* chasseur

Valmont So he grasped what was going on, did he?
Azolan Oh, yes, sir. I was watching him and he was watching you.
Valmont I just hope he was better at understanding what was happening than he was at shadowing me; I sat down for a rest on the way and he was trampling about behind some bush, making so much noise I had a good mind to give him a legful of small shot. Except then I suppose he'd have had even more trouble keeping up.
Azolan He knew what you were doing; and after you'd gone he talked to the family.
Valmont I must say the family was very well chosen.
Azolan Thank you, sir.
Valmont Solidly respectable, gratifyingly tearful, no suspiciously pretty girls. Well done.
Azolan I do my best for you, sir.
Valmont And not even unduly expensive. Fifty-six livres to save an entire family from ruin, that seems a genuine bargain.
Azolan These days, my lord, you can find half a dozen like that, any village in the country.

Valmont Really? I must say, it's no longer a mystery to me why people fall so easily into the habit of charitable enterprises. All that humble gratitude. It was most affecting.

Azolan Certainly brought a tear to my eye, sir.

Valmont How are you getting on with the maid?

Azolan Julie? Tell you the truth, it's been a bit boring. If I wasn't so anxious to keep your lordship abreast, I think I'd only have bothered the once. I'm not sure she doesn't feel the same, but, you know, what else is there to do in the country?

Valmont Yes, it wasn't so much the details of your intimacy I was after, it was whether she's agreed to bring me Madame de Tourvel's letters and do you think she'll keep her mouth shut?

Azolan She won't steal the letters, sir.

Valmont She won't?

Azolan You know better than me, sir, it's easy enough making them do what they want to do; it's trying to get them to do what you want them to do, that's what gives you a headache.

Valmont And them, as often as not.

Azolan As for keeping her mouth shut, I haven't asked her to keep her mouth shut, because that's the one thing most likely to give her the idea of opening it.

Valmont You may well be right. But look, Madame de Tourvel told me she'd been warned about me: that means some officious friend must have written to her about me. I need to know who.

Azolan I shouldn't worry about all that, if I was you, sir. If she's interested enough to have you followed, I'd say it was only a matter of time.

Valmont Do you think so?

Azolan Anyway, apparently she keeps her letters in her pockets.

Valmont I wish I knew how to pick pockets. Why don't our parents ever teach us anything useful? (*Pause, as he considers*) Where do you and Julie meet?

Azolan Oh, in my room, sir.

Valmont And is she coming tonight?

Azolan Afraid so.

Valmont Then I think I may have to burst in on you. See if blackmail will succeed better than bribery. About two o'clock suit you? I don't want to embarrass you, will that give you enough time?

Azolan Ample, sir.

Valmont Good.

Azolan Then you won't have to pay her, sir, will you?

Valmont Oh, I think if she delivers, we can afford to be generous, don't you?

Azolan It's your money, sir.

Valmont Don't worry, I shan't overlook your contribution.

Azolan Well, that's very decent of you, sir.

Valmont looks up at the sound of approaching female voices. He turns back to Azolan

Valmont Off you go, then. See you at two.

Azolan Right, sir. I'll be sure to arrange her so she can't say she's there to borrow a clothes brush.

Azolan leaves by one door as Mme de Rosemonde and Mme de Tourvel arrive by another. Mme de Rosemonde is eighty-four, arthritic but lively, intelligent and sympathetic; and Mme de Tourvel is a handsome woman of twenty-two, dressed not as Merteuil described, but in an elegantly plain linen gown. She is clearly in a state of considerable excitement

Rosemonde Here he is. I said he would be here.

Valmont rises to greet them. Tourvel cannot help reacting to his presence

Valmont Ladies.

Rosemonde Madame de Tourvel has some mystery to reveal to us.

Tourvel To you, Madame, to you.

Valmont Oh, well, then, perhaps I should go for a walk.

Tourvel No, no, it, it concerns you as well, I mean, it particularly concerns you. In fact, I must begin by asking you some questions.

Valmont Very well. Just let me help my aunt to her chair.

Valmont installs Mme de Rosemonde in her armchair, then turns his attention back to Mme de Tourvel

Valmont Now.

Tourvel Where did you go this morning, Monsieur?

Valmont Well, as you know, I was up early to go out hunting.

Tourvel And did you succeed in making a kill this time?

Valmont No, I've had the most wretched luck ever since I arrived here. Also I'm a terrible shot.

Tourvel But on this occasion, Monsieur le Vicomte, what exactly was it you were hunting?

Valmont I'm sorry, I'm afraid I don't quite follow ...

Tourvel You may as well own up, Monsieur, I know where you were this morning.

Rosemonde I think it's time somebody explained to me what's going on.

Tourvel Georges, my footman, just happened to be in the village earlier today ...

Valmont I do hope you haven't been listening to servants' gossip.

Tourvel I can see Monsieur de Valmont is determined not to tell you, so I shall have to. There's a family in the village, the man has been ill, he found himself not able to pay his taxes this year. So this morning the bailiff arrived to seize their few sticks of furniture. Whereupon your nephew, whose valet had been making enquiries in the village to see if anyone was suffering from particular hardship, arrived, paid off the family's debts and added a generous contribution to help them back on their feet again.

Rosemonde Is this true, my dear?

Valmont Well, I ... it's simply ... yes.

Mme de Rosemonde rises to her feet and spreads out her arms

Rosemonde You dear boy, come and let me give you a hug!

Valmont crosses to her and they embrace. Then Valmont turns and advances towards Mme de Tourvel, smiling radiantly, his arms outstretched. A spasm of panic crosses her face but she has no choice but to submit to the embrace: Valmont squeezes her powerfully. Then he releases her and, as she looks at him, ashen and mesmerized, he turns aside, wiping away a surreptitious tear

It's so like you to make a secret of something like that.

In the ensuing silence, Mme de Tourvel moves across to the tapestry frame, and picks up the already-threaded needle. But her hands are shaking so badly, she has to put it down again

We must visit this family in the morning, my dear, to see if we can help in any other way.

Tourvel Yes, I'd like that.

Valmont Do sit down, aunt.

Rosemonde No, I must try to find Monsieur le Curé. I shan't be long, but I do want to tell him about this before he leaves, he'll be so pleased.

Mme de Rosemonde bustles out of the room, and a long silence ensues

Mme de Tourvel makes a renewed and determined effort to get to grips with her tapestry; Valmont finds a chair facing her, watches and waits. The light is beginning to die. Finally, Mme de Tourvel, struggling for composure, feels compelled to break the silence

Tourvel I can't understand how someone whose instincts are so generous could lead such a dissolute life.

Valmont I'm afraid you have an exaggerated idea both of my generosity and of my depravity. If I knew who'd given you such a dire account of me, I might be able to defend myself; since I don't, let me make a confession: I'm afraid the key to the paradox lies in a certain weakness of character.

Tourvel I don't see how so thoughtful an act of charity could be described as weak.

Valmont This appalling reputation of mine, you see, there is some justification for it. I've spent my life surrounded by immoral people; I've allowed myself to be influenced by them and sometimes even taken pride in outshining them. Whereas, in this case, I've simply fallen under a quite opposite kind of influence: yours.

Tourvel You mean you wouldn't have done it ...?

Valmont Not without your example, no. It was by way of an innocent tribute to your goodness.

There's a pause, during which Mme de Tourvel, uncertain how to react, abandons her tapestry, hovers indecisively for a second and then sits, perching on the edge of a chaise-longue

You see how weak I am? I promised myself I was never going to tell you. It's just, looking at you ...

Tourvel Monsieur.

Valmont You needn't worry, I have no illicit intentions, I wouldn't dream of insulting you. But I do love you. I adore you. (*He's across the room in an instant, drops to one knee in front of her and takes her hands in his*) Please help me!

Mme de Tourvel wrenches her hands free and bursts into tears

What is it?

Tourvel I'm so unhappy! (*She buries her face in her hands, sobbing*)

For an instant, a shadow of a smile twitches across Valmont's face, before he speaks in a voice on the edge of tears

Valmont But why?

Tourvel Will you leave me now?

Valmont rises and moves away across the room, ostensibly making an effort to control himself

Valmont I shouldn't have said anything, I know I shouldn't, I'm sorry. But really, you have nothing to fear. Nothing at all. Tell me what to do, show me how to behave, I'll do anything you say.

Mme de Tourvel manages to control herself and looks up at him

Tourvel I thought the least I could hope for was that you would respect me.

Valmont But I do, of course I do!

Tourvel Then forget all this, don't say another word, you've offended me deeply, it's unforgivable.

Valmont I thought you might at least give me some credit for being honest.

Tourvel On the contrary, this confirms everything I've been told about you. I'm beginning to think you may well have planned the whole exercise.

Valmont When I came to visit my aunt, I had no idea you were here: not that it would have disturbed me in the slightest if I had known. You see, up until then, I'd only ever experienced desire. Love, never.

Tourvel That's enough.

Valmont No, no, you made an accusation, you must allow me the opportunity to defend myself. Now, you were there when my aunt asked me to stay a little longer, and at that time I only agreed in deference to her, although I was already by no means unaware of your beauty.

Tourvel Monsieur . . .

Valmont No, the point is, all this has nothing to do with your beauty. As I got to know you, I began to realize that beauty is the least of your qualities. I became fascinated by your goodness, I was drawn in by it, I didn't understand what was happening to me, and it was only when I began to feel actual physical pain every time you left the room, that it finally dawned on me: I was in love, for the first time in my life. I knew it was hopeless, of course, but that didn't matter to me, because it wasn't like it always had been, it wasn't that I wanted to have you, no. All I wanted was to deserve you.

Mme de Tourvel rises decisively to her feet

Tourvel I really will have to leave you, Monsieur, you seem determined to persist with a line of argument you must know I ought not to listen to and I don't want to hear.
Valmont No, no, please, sit down, sit down. I've already told you, I'll do anything you say.

Silence. They watch each other. Eventually, Mme de Tourvel sits down again

Tourvel There's only one thing I would like you to do for me.
Valmont What? What is it?
Tourvel But I don't see how I can ask you, I'm not even sure if I want to put myself in the position of being beholden to you.
Valmont Oh, please, no, I insist, if you're good enough to give me an opportunity to do something you want, anything, it's I who will be beholden to you.

Mme de Tourvel looks at Valmont for a moment with characteristic openness

Tourvel Very well, then. I would like you to leave this house.

There flashes momentarily across Valmont's face the expression of a chess champion who has just lost his queen

Valmont I don't see why that should be necessary
Tourvel Let's just say you've spent your life making it necessary.

By now, Valmont has recovered his equilibrium; and thought very fast

Valmont Well then, of course, whatever you say. I couldn't possibly refuse you.

It's Mme de Tourvel's turn to be surprised

Will you allow me to give my aunt, say, twenty-four hours' notice?
Tourvel Well, yes, naturally.
Valmont I shall find something in my mail tomorrow morning which obliges me to return at once to Paris.
Tourvel Thank you, I'd be very grateful.
Valmont Perhaps I might be so bold as to ask a favour in return.

Mme de Tourvel frowns, hesitating

I think it would only be just to let me know which of your friends has blackened my name.
Tourvel You know very well that's impossible, Monsieur. If friends of mine have warned me against you, they've done so purely in my own interest and I could hardly reward them with betrayal, could I? I must say, you devalue your generous offer if you want to use it as a bargaining point.

Valmont Very well, I withdraw the request. I hope you won't think I'm bargaining if I ask you to let me write to you.

Tourvel Well ...

Valmont And hope that you will do me the kindness of answering my letters.

Tourvel I'm not sure a correspondence with you is something a woman of honour could permit herself.

Valmont So you're determined to refuse all my suggestions, however respectable?

Tourvel I didn't say that.

Valmont I really don't see how you could possibly be harmed by conceding me this very minor but, as far as I'm concerned, vitally important consolation.

Tourvel I would welcome the chance to prove to you that what motivates me in this is not hatred or resentment, but ...

Valmont But what?

But Mme de Tourvel seems unable to find a satisfactory answer to this. And, moving as suddenly and swiftly as before, Valmont again crosses the room, drops to one knee and takes her hand. She struggles to free it

Tourvel For God's sake, Monsieur, please, leave me alone!

Valmont I only want to say what I hardly thought it would be possible for me to say to you: goodbye.

Valmont kisses Mme de Tourvel's hand. She submits briefly, her expression anguished, then begins to struggle again, whereupon he releases her instantly, rises to his feet and bows

I'll write soon.

Valmont hurries away into the darkness, just failing to muffle a discreet sob. Mme de Tourvel is left alone, rooted to the chaise-longue. She looks terrified

SCENE 3

A couple of days later. The middle of the night

A bedroom in a house on the outskirts of Paris which belongs to Émilie, a courtesan. She's in bed with Valmont, lying in his arms, her eyes flashing in the candlelight. He seems lost in thought. Émilie shifts her position and he smiles down at her

Valmont I thought the Dutch were supposed to be famous for their capacity for alcohol.

Émilie Three bottles of burgundy and a bottle of cognac would finish anybody.

Valmont Did he drink that much?

Émilie You were pouring.

Valmont I hope you're not missing him.

Émilie Don't be silly. I just don't think it was necessary to bundle him into your carriage.

Valmont Man in that condition, I thought it best to send him back to his house.

Émilie This is his house.

Valmont Oh. I thought it was your house.

Émilie He owns it. I just live in it. And he's so rarely in France. Seems a shame. (*She grins broadly*)

Valmont Oh, well, I'm sure my coachman will use his imagination.

Émilie I'm sure, since you're perfectly aware of the position and have no doubt given him explicit instructions, he won't have to.

Valmont Explicit instructions?

Émilie Yes.

Silence

Valmont I must say, Émilie, I do think it's the height of bad manners to talk about some foreigner when you're in bed with me. I think some appropriate punishment is called for. Turn over.

Émilie hesitates, looking up at Valmont for a moment. Then she breaks into a smile

Émilie All right. (*She does so, looking up at Valmont expectantly*)

Valmont Now, do you have pen, ink and writing paper?

Émilie is puzzled. After a while, she answers

Émilie Yes, over there, in the bureau. Why?

Instead of answering, Valmont gets out of bed, crosses the room, finds what he's looking for in the bureau and brings it back to the bed. He puts down the pen and inkwell carefully, twitches back the bedclothes, spreads a sheet of paper across the small of Émilie's back, arranges himself comfortably and reaches for the pen

Valmont Now don't move.

Émilie is still puzzled. But she submits graciously enough. Valmont begins to write

"My dear Madame de Tourvel ... I have just come ... to my desk ..."

Émilie understands now. She turns her head to smile up at Valmont

Don't move, I said. (*He resumes*) "... in the middle of a stormy night, during which I have been tossed from exaltation to exhaustion and back again. The position in which I find myself as I write has made me more than ever aware of the power of love. I can scarcely control myself sufficiently to put my thoughts in order; but despite these torments I guarantee that at this moment I am far happier than you. I hope one day you may feel the kind of disturbance afflicting me now: meanwhile please excuse me while I take steps to calm what I can only describe as a mounting excitement." (*He moves aside paper, pen and inkwell and leans back to nuzzle Émilie, who hasn't moved*)   We'll finish it later, shall we?

The Lights fade to Black-out

SCENE 4

Ten days later. A September afternoon

Valmont is taking tea with la Marquise de Merteuil in her grand salon

Merteuil It sounds to me as if you made a serious tactical error. Shouldn't you have taken Madame de Tourvel there and then on the chaise-longue?

Valmont I was expecting my aunt and the curé to appear at any moment.

Merteuil Well, it would have been the most interesting thing to happen to them for years.

Valmont No, it wasn't at all the moment: I want her to surrender, but not before she's put up a fight.

Merteuil She seems to be: she's succeeded in getting rid of you altogether.

Valmont But I got her to agree to let me write to her.

Merteuil Well, in the unlikely event of her defences being pierced by your eloquence, you're not going to be there to take advantage of it, are you? And by the following day they'll be back in full repair.

Valmont Naturally, writing to someone is a poor substitute, but since I really had no choice in the matter, at least I've found a way to keep the thing alive.

Merteuil Perhaps.

Valmont I know you're incurably sceptical, but for me, with a woman, this is by far the best stage, it's what men talk about all the time but hardly ever experience, the real intoxication: when you know she loves you, but you're still not quite certain of victory.

Merteuil You know she loves you, then?

Valmont Oh, yes. I left my man there to keep an eye on things and a hand on the maid, who's been most co-operative since I caught them in bed together: and he tells me that when my first letter arrived, she took it to her room and sat turning it over for hours, sighing and weeping. So it seems a reasonable enough conclusion.

Merteuil says nothing, but her expression remains dubious

And the maid helped us to another discovery which might interest you.

Merteuil Oh, yes?

Valmont Can you guess who it was who kept writing to my beauty, warn-ing her to steer clear of the world's vilest pervert, namely me? Your damned cousin, the Volanges bitch.

Merteuil bursts out laughing

It's all very well for you to laugh, she's set me back at least a month.

Merteuil It's not that.

Valmont She wanted me away from Madame de Tourvel: well, now I am and I intend to make her suffer for it. Your plan to ruin her daughter: are you making any progress? Is there anything I can do to help? I'm entirely at your disposal.

Merteuil Well, as a matter of fact, my dear Vicomte, your presence here today forms part of my plan. I'm expecting Danceny at any moment and I want you to help me stiffen his resolve, if that's the phrase. And then I've arranged a little scene I hope you may find entertaining: yes, I'm sure you will.

Valmont Is that all you're going to say?

Merteuil Yes, I think so.

Valmont Has Danceny not been a great success?

Merteuil He's been disastrous. Like most intellectuals, he's intensely stupid. He really is a most incompetent boy. Charming, but hopeless.

Valmont You'd better bring me up to date.

Merteuil Well, I've become extremely thick with little Cécile. We go to my box at the Opéra and chatter away all evening. I'm really quite jealous of whoever's in store for her. She has a certain innate duplicity which is going to stand her in very good stead. She has no character and no morals, she's altogether delicious.

Valmont But what's happened?

Merteuil She and Danceny are head over heels in love. It started when she asked me if it would be wrong for her to write to him. First I said yes and later I said no, it would be all right, as long as she showed me both sides of the correspondence. Then I arranged a meeting, but Danceny was so paralysed with chivalry, he didn't lay a finger on her. All his energies go into writing her poems of great ingenuity and minimum impact. I tried to ginger things up by telling her it was Gercourt her mother intended her to marry. She was shocked enough to discover he was a geriatric of thirty-six, but by the time I'd finished describing him, she couldn't have hated him more if they'd been married ten years. Then, the first major setback: she told her confessor and he took a very strong line. So she severed relations with Danceny and spent all her time praying to be able to forget him, a pleasantly self-contradictory exercise. He remained abject throughout. The only thing I could do was to organize a rendezvous for them to say goodbye to one another and hope for the best. And after all that, what do I find? Danceny has managed to hold her hand for five seconds, and when asked to let go, to Cécile's extreme annoyance, he does. You really have to put some backbone into him. Afterwards the little one said to me, "Oh, Madame, I wish you were Danceny": and, do you know, just for a minute, I wished I was.

Valmont I often wonder how you managed to invent yourself.

Merteuil I had no choice, did I, I'm a woman. Women are obliged to be far more skilful than men, because who ever wastes time cultivating inessential skills? You think you put as much ingenuity into winning us as we put into losing: well, it's debatable, I suppose, but from then on, you hold every ace in the pack. You can ruin us whenever the fancy takes you: all we can achieve by denouncing you is to enhance your prestige. We can't even get rid of you when we want to: we're compelled to unstitch, painstakingly, what you would just cut through. We either have to devise some way of making you want to leave us, so you'll feel too guilty to harm us; or find a reliable means of blackmail: otherwise you can destroy our reputation and our life with a few well-chosen words. So of course I had to invent: not only myself, but ways of escape no one else has ever thought of, not even I, because I had to be fast enough on my feet to know how to improvise. And I've succeeded, because I always knew I was born to dominate your sex and avenge my own.

Valmont Yes; but what I asked you was how.

Merteuil When I came out into society, I'd already realized that the role I was condemned to, namely to keep quiet and do as I was told, gave me the perfect opportunity to listen and pay attention: not to what people told me, which was naturally of no interest, but to whatever it was they were trying to hide. I practised detachment. I learned how to smile pleasantly while, under the table, I stuck a fork into the back of my hand. I became not merely impenetrable, but a virtuoso of deceit. Needless to say, at that stage nobody told me anything: and it wasn't pleasure I was after, it was knowledge. But when, in the interests of furthering that knowledge, I told my confessor I'd done "everything", his reaction was so appalled, I began to get a sense of how extreme pleasure might be. No sooner had I made this discovery than my mother announced my marriage: so I was able to contain my curiosity and arrived in Monsieur de Merteuil's arms a virgin. All in all, Merteuil gave me little cause for complaint: and the minute I began to find him something of a nuisance, he very tactfully died. I used my year of mourning to complete my studies: I consulted the strictest moralists to learn how to appear; philosophers to find out what to think; and novelists to see what I could get away with. And finally I was well placed to perfect my techniques.

Valmont Describe them.

Merteuil Only flirt with those you intend to refuse: then you acquire a reputation for invincibility, whilst slipping safely away with the lover of your choice. A poor choice is less dangerous than an obvious choice. Never write letters. Get them to write letters. Always be sure they think they're the only one. Win or die.

Valmont smiles. He looks at Merteuil for a moment

Valmont These principles are infallible, are they?

Merteuil When I want a man, I have him; when he wants to tell, he finds he can't. That's the whole story.

Valmont And was that our story?

Merteuil pauses before answering

Merteuil I wanted you before we'd even met. My self-esteem demanded it.

Then, when you began to pursue me ... I wanted you so badly. It's the only one of my notions has ever got the better of me. Single combat.

Valmont Thank you ...

Valmont is interrupted by the arrival of Merteuil's major-domo, escorting the Chevalier Danceny, a Knight of Malta, an eager and handsome young man of about twenty. Danceny hurries over and bows to kiss Merteuil's hand. Then he acknowledges Valmont. The Major-domo exits

Danceny Vicomte.

Valmont My dear young man. How good to see you again.

Danceny turns back to Merteuil, speaks a trifle breathlessly

Danceny I'm sorry to be late, Madame.

Merteuil Very nearly too late. (*But looking up at Danceny's sincerely repentant expression, she softens*) As you know, Mademoiselle de Volanges ...

Danceny It gives me such pleasure to hear her name spoken, Madame.

Merteuil Yes, yes, quite. As I was saying, Mademoiselle de Volanges has done me the honour of making me her confidante and counsellor in this matter which concerns you both.

Danceny She could hardly have chosen more wisely.

Merteuil Yes, well, be that as it may, I felt very strongly that in this situation, which is exceedingly delicate, you too might find it beneficial to be able to confide in someone sympathetic, a person of experience: and the Vicomte de Valmont, who is known to you as well as being an old friend of mine and a man of unswerving discretion, seems to me an ideal choice. And should you agree, he's very kindly consented to devote himself to your interests.

A frown crosses Valmont's face: but by the time Danceny, who for his part seems slightly flustered by this offer, turns to him, it's vanished

Danceny Well ...

Valmont Perhaps it is my reputation which is causing you to hesitate: if so, I think I can assure you that a man's own mistakes are not necessarily a guide to his faculty for objective judgement.

Danceny No, of course not, I certainly wouldn't have the impudence, no, it's ... the fact is, this is not a conventional intrigue with the aim of ... that's to say, my love and respect ...

Valmont We're not dealing, you mean, with a frivolous coquette or a bored wife?

Danceny Precisely. A person like Mademoiselle de Volanges must be treated with the utmost consideration. And my own position has certain weaknesses, of which I'm only too bitterly aware. Her great fortune, for example, compared to my own precarious condition ...

Valmont Naturally, there would be no excuse for trying to manoeuvre her into such a pass that she would be forced to marry you, that would be quite wrong.

Danceny You do understand how I feel.

Merteuil Of course he does, what did I tell you?

Danceny You see, I'm quite happy with things as they are, as long as she consents to see me, to continue with the music lessons.

Valmont Ah, the music lessons.

The Major-domo reappears and crosses the room to murmur to Merteuil. She gives him some instructions in an undertone and he bows and leaves

In any case, I have absolutely no wish to press my attentions on you . . .

Danceny No, please . . .

Valmont But do rest assured that I am honoured to be at your disposal.

Danceny The honour, Monsieur, is entirely mine, and any contact with you would be a privilege. Perhaps you would care to . . .

Merteuil I'm sorry to interrupt you, Chevalier, but I'm afraid you must leave. Madame de Volanges has just been announced. You see now why I was concerned at your late arrival.

Danceny Maybe this would be a good opportunity for me to pay my respects and hope to . . .

Merteuil I really think at this juncture, Monsieur Danceny, it would be prudent for you not to be found here. That is if you want me to be of any effective assistance in the future.

A Footman enters during the above

Danceny Of course, whatever you think fit.

Merteuil Goodbye, Chevalier. My man will show you to a side exit.

Danceny kisses Merteuil's hand in hurried farewell

Valmont takes Danceny's arm as he crosses to the door

Valmont I have to go to Versailles tomorrow, I don't know if you'd care to accompany me.

Danceny I'd like that very much.

Valmont Good, I'll send a carriage for you at nine.

Danceny vanishes with the Footman

Valmont turns back to Merteuil

So this is the scene you have planned for me?

Merteuil If you'd care to go behind the screen (*She indicates a screen in a corner of the room, a trace of anxious impatience in her voice*)

Valmont I think you might have consulted me before offering my services as general factotum to that exasperating boy. I don't find lovers' complaints remotely entertaining outside of the Opéra.

Merteuil I was sure that if anyone could help him . . .

Valmont Help? He doesn't need help, he needs hindrances: if he has to climb over enough of them, he might inadvertently fall on top of her.

Merteuil I'll see what I can do: now, Vicomte, the screen.

Valmont starts moving towards it, then hesitates

Valmont Are you sure I shouldn't confront her? Give her some evidence
for those rude letters?

Merteuil Quick.

*Valmont moves swiftly and is only just behind the screen in time not to be
seen by Mme de Volanges, as she's shown in by the Major-domo*

*Merteuil, who has assumed a grave expression, rises to greet Mme de
Volanges, kissing her on both cheeks*

Volanges Your note said it was urgent ...

Merteuil It's days now, I haven't been able to think about anything else,
I couldn't decide what to do for the best. Finally I saw there was no
escaping the fact it was my plain duty to tell you. Please sit down.

*Mme de Volanges, now decidedly uneasy, does so, as Merteuil paces to and
fro, looking anguished*

As you know, in recent weeks, Cécile has been kind enough to accept my
friendship and, I believe, bestow on me her own.

Volanges Yes, of course, she's devoted to you.

Merteuil This is what makes this duty doubly difficult to perform.

Volanges This has something to do with Cécile?

Merteuil I may be wrong; I pray Heaven I am.

Merteuil pauses again; by now, Mme de Volanges is thoroughly alarmed

Volanges Go on.

Merteuil takes a deep breath

Merteuil I have reason to believe that a, how can I describe it, a dangerous
liaison has sprung up between your daughter and the Chevalier Danceny.

*Silence. Mme de Volanges is dumbfounded and so, should he be visible behind
the screen, is Valmont. But it takes only a few seconds for Mme de Volanges
to recover her equilibrium*

Volanges No, no, that's completely absurd. Cécile is still a child, she understands nothing of these things; and Danceny is an entirely respectable
young man.

Merteuil If you were to be right, no one would be happier than I.

Volanges Naturally, they've never been together unchaperoned, generally
by me and often by you.

Merteuil Precisely, that's when I first formed the impression that something was passing between them: the way they looked at each other.

Volanges I'm sure it's merely their feeling for the music.

Merteuil Perhaps so. But there was one other thing. Tell me, does Cécile
have a great many correspondents?

Volanges She writes, I suppose, an average number of letters. Relatives,
friends from the convent ... Why?

Merteuil I went into her room at the beginning of this week, I simply
knocked and entered without waiting for a reply, and she was stuffing

a letter into the left-hand drawer of her bureau, in which, I couldn't help noticing, there seemed to be a large number of similar letters.

Silence. Then Mme de Volanges rises to her feet

Volanges I'm most grateful to you. I'll see myself out.

Merteuil I hope you don't think me interfering.

Volanges Not at all.

Merteuil And do I hope, if, God forbid, you do discover anything compromising, you won't tell Cécile it was I who was responsible. I would hate to forfeit her trust, and if there is to be a period of difficulty, I would like to think my advice might be of some use to her.

Volanges Of course.

Merteuil rings. Mme de Volanges stands there, still in a state of mild shock

Merteuil Would you think it impertinent if I were to make another suggestion?

Volanges No, no.

Merteuil If my recollection is correct, I overheard you saying to the Vicomte de Valmont that his aunt had invited you to stay at her château.

Volanges She has, yes, repeatedly.

Merteuil A spell in the country might be the very thing until all this blows over.

Volanges If what you tell me has any truth in it, I may very well send her back to the convent.

Merteuil Wouldn't it be better to threaten that as a punishment if there's any resumption of relations?

Volanges Perhaps. I can't believe you're right about this.

Merteuil Let's hope not.

The Major-domo arrives and Merteuil beckons him over

Mme de Volanges meanwhile is lost in thought. She looks up, frowning

Volanges Isn't the Vicomte staying there at the moment?

Merteuil I understand he's returned to Paris. (*She embraces Mme de Volanges warmly*) I expect I've imagined the whole thing and tomorrow we'll be able to laugh at my stupidity. If so, I hope you'll be able to forgive me.

Volanges My dear, I shall always be more than grateful for your concern. (*They part*)

Mme de Volanges moves slowly out of the room, bowed down with care, following the Major-domo

Because of her progress, Valmont emerges from behind the screen before she's disappeared, to Merteuil's alarm. But Mme de Volanges doesn't look back and Valmont can't resist making faces at her retreating back, causing Merteuil to hiss at him

Merteuil Stop it.

Valmont So, you understand I've returned to Paris?

Merteuil You asked for hindrances.

Valmont You're a genuinely wicked woman.

Merteuil And you wanted a chance to make my cousin suffer.

Valmont I can't resist you.

Merteuil I've made it easy for you.

Valmont But all this is most inconvenient: the Comtesse de Beaulieu has invited me to stay.

Merteuil Well, you'll have to put her off.

Valmont The Comtesse has promised me extensive use of her gardens. It seems her husband's fingers are not as green as they once were.

Merteuil Maybe not. But from what I hear, all his friends are gardeners.

Valmont Is that so?

Merteuil You want your revenge: I want my revenge. I'm afraid there's really only one place you can go.

Valmont Back to Auntie, eh?

Merteuil Back to Auntie. Where you can also pursue that other matter. You have some evidence to procure, have you not?

Valmont Don't you think it would be a generous gesture, show a proper confidence in my abilities, I mean, to take that evidence for granted, and ...?

Merteuil I need it in writing, Vicomte.

Valmont gives Merteuil his most charming smile, but it leaves her unmoved

And now you must leave me.

Valmont Must I? Why?

Merteuil Because I'm hungry.

Valmont Yes, I've quite an appetite myself.

Merteuil Then go home and eat.

Silence. Then Valmont crosses to Merteuil and lingeringly kisses her hand

In writing.

Valmont smiles, turns and strides away

SCENE 5

A week later. After lunch. The salon in Mme de Rosemonde's château

Mme de Tourvel is stretched out on the chaise-longue, ashen; Cécile sits in the window, working at her tapestry: Mme de Rosemonde and Mme de Volanges sit at the card table; and only Valmont is on his feet, moving around the room, his eye roving from Mme de Tourvel to Cécile and back again

Rosemonde You'll be pleased to hear, my dear, that Armand is on his feet again and back at work.

Valmont Who?

Rosemonde Monsieur Armand, you remember, whose family you helped
so generously

Valmont Oh, yes.

*Valmont comes to rest and sits down, his eye fixed now on Mme de Tourvel.
When she looks at him, he looks away for a few seconds at Cécile, and is
gratified to notice, when he looks back at Mme de Tourvel, that she's still
looking at him, although she looks away again, in some confusion, the minute
he catches her out*

Rosemonde We've been keeping an eye on things while you've been away:
I must say he never ceases to sing your praises. (*She turns to Mme de
Volanges*) When my nephew was last staying here, we discovered quite
by chance that he had been down to the village and—

Valmont suddenly rises to his feet, still staring at Mme de Tourvel

Valmont Are you feeling all right, Madame?

Momentary confusion

I'm sorry to interrupt you, Aunt, it seemed to me all of a sudden that
Madame de Tourvel didn't look at all well.

Tourvel I'm ... no, I'm quite all right.

*Mme de Rosemonde and Mme de Volanges get to their feet and hurry
towards Mme de Tourvel, who now does look genuinely ill, despite her feeble
protests*

*As they bear down on her, Valmont turns towards Cécile, who's still sitting,
needle poised, in the window, and deftly throws a letter into her lap. She's so
amazed by this, she sits there for a moment, gaping; until she grasps the
significance of Valmont's impatient gestures, tosses her tapestry aside and
stuffs the letter in her pocket. Finally, again at a gesture from Valmont, she
moves towards the chaise-longue, exhibiting polite concern and standing, next
to Valmont, at a respectful distance from the centre of attention, Mme de
Tourvel*

Rosemonde You do look dreadfully pale, me dear.

Tourvel I'm all right.

Volanges Perhaps you need some air. Do you feel constricted in any way?

Tourvel No, really ...

Valmont I feel sure Madame de Volanges is right, as usual. A turn around
the grounds, perhaps.

Rosemonde Yes, yes, a little walk in the garden, it's not too cool, I think.

Tourvel Well, perhaps ...

Volanges Come along, my dear, we'll all accompany you.

Tourvel I'll be quite happy on my own.

Valmont You'll have to excuse me, ladies, but I think you're right to insist
on chaperoning Madame.

Mme de Tourvel is wrong-footed by this: she frowns slightly in puzzlement and allows a shawl to be wrapped around her shoulders, as she's propelled towards the french windows by Mme de Rosemonde and Mme de Volanges

Rosemonde Fresh air will do you the world of good.

Volanges The meal was somewhat heavy, perhaps ...

Rosemonde I don't believe that can be the cause, Solange is an excellent cook ...

During this exchange, Cécile has gathered up her shawl and made to follow the others. As she's spreading it across her shoulders, however, she's startled to find it tugged away from her by Valmont, who drops it on a chair and simultaneously murmurs to her between clenched teeth

Valmont Come back for it.

Cécile frowns at him for a moment, then follows the still-clucking ladies, who are now supporting Mme de Tourvel on either side, out into the garden. Hiatus

Valmont moves around the room, apparently well pleased

Presently Cécile re-appears and stands hesitantly just inside the windows. Valmont picks up her shawl and strides towards her

I don't want to arouse suspicion, Mademoiselle, so I must be brief and I must ask you to pay close attention to what I say. As you've no doubt guessed, the letter I gave you is from our friend, the Chevalier Danceny.

Cécile Yes, I thought so, Monsieur.

Valmont And as I'm sure you're also aware, the handing-over of letters is a far from easy matter to accomplish. I can't very well create a diversion every day.

Cécile And Maman has taken away my paper and pens.

Valmont Right, now listen carefully: there are two large cupboards in the antechamber next to your room. In the left-hand cupboard, you will find a supply of paper, pens and ink.

Cécile Oh, thank you!

Valmont I suggest you return the Chevalier's letters to me, when you've read them, for safe-keeping.

Cécile Must I?

Valmont It would be wise. (*At this point, he produces a key from his waist-coat pocket*) Now, this key resembles the key to your bedroom, which I happen to know is kept in your mother's room, on the mantelpiece, tied with a blue ribbon. Take it, attach the blue ribbon to it and put it in the place of your bedroom key, which you will then bring to me. I'll be able to get a copy cut within two hours, I'll return you the original and you can put it back in your mother's room. Then I'll be able to collect your letters and deliver Danceny's without any complications.

Valmont hands the key to Cécile, who takes it dubiously

Oh, and on the shelf below the writing paper, you'll find a feather and a small bottle of oil, so that you can oil the lock and hinges on your bedroom door.

Cécile Are you sure, Monsieur, I'm not sure it would be right ...

Valmont How else are we going to manage this? Your mother never lets you out of her sight. You really must trust me, my dear.

Cécile Well, I know Monsieur Danceny has every confidence in you ....

Valmont Believe me, Mademoiselle, if there's one thing I can't abide, it's deceitfulness. It's only my very warm friendship with Danceny which would ever make me consider such methods.

Cécile smiles uncertainly and puts the key away. She stands there, obviously racked with indecision

And now I suggest you rejoin your mama and the others before they send out a search party.

Cécile Yes, Monsieur. Thank you, Monsieur.

Cécile turns and hurries back into the garden with her shawl

Valmont watches her go, thoughtful

Valmont My pleasure. (*He moves over to an armchair and sinks into it, picks up a book from the arm of the chair, finds his place and settles to read*)

The lights change. It's early evening now

Valmont, still reading, looks up as Mme de Tourvel comes into the room. She freezes as soon as she sees Valmont, who puts down his book and rises to his feet

I trust you're feeling a little better, Madame.

Tourvel If I had felt ill, Monsieur, it would not be difficult to guess who was responsible.

Valmont You can't mean me. Do you?

Tourvel You promised to leave here.

Valmont And I did.

Tourvel Then how can you be insensitive enough to return uninvited and without warning?

Valmont I find myself obliged to attend to some urgent business in the area: in which, moreover, my aunt is crucially involved.

Tourvel I only hope it can be dealt with promptly.

Mme de Tourvel cautiously moves closer to the centre of the room. As the conversation continues, Valmont contrives, imperceptibly, to manoeuvre himself between her and the door

Valmont Why are you so angry with me?

Tourvel I'm not angry. Although, since you gave me a solemn undertaking not to offend me when you wrote and then in your very first letter spoke of nothing but the disorders of love, I'm certainly entitled to be.

Valmont I was away almost three weeks and wrote to you only three times. Since I was quite unable to think about anything but you, some might say I showed heroic restraint.

Tourvel Not in so far as you persisted in writing about your love, despite my pleas for you not to do so.

Valmont It's true: I couldn't find the strength to obey you.

Tourvel You claim to think there's some connection between what you call love and happiness: I can't believe that there is.

Valmont In these circumstances, I agree. When the love is unrequited ...

Tourvel As it must be. You know it's impossible for me to reciprocate your feelings; and even if I did, it could only cause me suffering, without making you any the happier.

Valmont But what else could I have written to you about, other than my love? What else is there? I believe I've done everything you've asked of me.

Tourvel You've done nothing of the sort.

Valmont I left here when you wanted me to.

Tourvel And you came back.

Silence, as Valmont searches for a way forward, momentarily at a loss

I've offered you my friendship, Monsieur. It's the only thing I can give you: why can't you accept it?

Valmont I could pretend to: but that would be dishonest.

Tourvel You're not answering my question.

Valmont The man I used to be would have been content with friendship; and set about trying to turn it to his advantage. But I've changed now: and I can't conceal from you that I love you tenderly, passionately and above all, respectfully. So how am I to demote myself to the tepid position of friend?

Valmont's strategy has paid off, because at this moment Mme de Tourvel decides to leave the room and finds the way blocked

And in any case, you're no longer even pretending to show friendship.

Tourvel What do you mean?

Valmont Well, is this friendly?

Tourvel You can hardly expect me to stay here and listen to the expression of sentiments you know very well I can only find insulting.

Valmont I think you're misunderstanding me: I know you can bestow on me nothing more than your friendship, for which, by the way, I'm profoundly grateful. In the same way, I can feel nothing less for you than love. We both know this is the true position: can't we simply acknowledge it? I don't see why recognition of the truth should lose me your friendship. Openness and honesty scarcely deserve to be punished, don't you agree?

Tourvel You are adept, Monsieur, at framing questions which preclude the answer no. Your honesty or otherwise is not at issue. The point is, surely, that I was weak enough to be persuaded to grant you a favour you should never have obtained; and furthermore I did this under certain conditions, not a single one of which you have observed. Naturally, I feel you've exploited my good faith.

Valmont What can I say to reassure you? How can you be afraid of me when, because I love you, your happiness is far more important to me than my own? You've made me a better person: you mustn't now undo your handiwork.

Tourvel I've no wish to: but I must ask whether you're going to leave the room or let me pass.

Valmont But why?

Tourvel Because I find this conversation distressing. I can't seem to make you understand what I mean; and I've no wish to hear what you invariably get round to saying.

Valmont Very well, I shall leave you in possession of the field.

Tourvel Thank you.

Valmont But look: I shall expedite my business, as you ask. But we are to be living under the same roof, at least for a few days; could we not contrive to tolerate it when fate throws us together? Surely we don't have to try to avoid each other?

Silence. Valmont waits

Tourvel Of course not. Providing you adhere to my few simple rules.

Valmont I shall obey you in this as in everything. I wish you knew me well enough to recognize how much you've changed me. My friends in Paris remarked on it at once. I've become the soul of consideration, charitable, conscientious, more celibate than a monk ...

Tourvel More celibate?

Valmont Well, you know, the stories one hears in Paris. (*Pause*) It's all due to your influence, I have you to thank for it. And now, good evening. (*He bows deep and turns away, begins moving towards the door*)

Tourvel Monsieur ...?

Valmont What?

Mme de Tourvel looks at Valmont for a moment, troubled; then shakes her head

Tourvel Nothing.

Valmont turns away, permits himself a private smile and leaves

Mme de Tourvel stands for a long time, not moving, locked in some personal struggle

SCENE 6

A fortnight later. The middle of the night. Cécile's bedroom in the château. Darkness

Cécile is fast asleep. After a while, there's the sound of a key in the lock. It operates smoothly and Valmont lets himself quietly into the room. He's wearing a dressing-gown and carrying a dark-lantern. He crosses to the bed and stands for a moment, contemplating the still-sleeping Cécile. He puts the lantern down carefully and, after some thought, leans forward and very gently eases back the covers. Disturbed, she stirs but still doesn't wake. Valmont puts a hand across her mouth. Her eyes open, wide and staring. Valmont smiles down at her and speaks in a whisper

Valmont Nothing to worry about.

Valmont removes his hand; Cécile continues to gape at him

Cécile Have you ... have you brought a letter?
Valmont No. Oh, no.
Cécile Then what ...?

Instead of answering, Valmont leans over to kiss her. There's a brief, fierce struggle, in which Cécile successfully defends herself from the kiss, but is taken entirely by surprise when Valmont plunges a hand up inside her night-dress. Her eyes widen in horror, but her cry is instantly stifled as Valmont's other hand clamps down on her mouth. She writhes determinedly for a moment, succeeds in freeing her head and dives across the bed to reach for the bell-pull. Valmont dives on to the bed in his turn, grasping her wrist just in time. They grapple fiercely and silently for a moment, until he manages to subdue her

Valmont You mustn't do that. What are you going to tell your mother
      when she arrives? How will you explain the fact that I have your key?
      If I tell her I'm here at your invitation, I have a feeling she'll believe me.

Valmont's hand is back in position now, and they're lying side by side on the bed

Cécile What do you want?
Valmont Well, I don't know, what do you think?
Cécile No, please, don't. Please.
Valmont All right. I just want you to give me a kiss.
Cécile A kiss?
Valmont That's all.
Cécile And then will you go?
Valmont Then I'll go.
Cécile Promise?
Valmont Whatever you say.

Cécile flops back on the pillow, with a slight groan and speaks, almost inau-dibly

Cécile All right.

Without removing his hand, Valmont leans over Cécile and gives her a long kiss. After a while he pulls away, but makes no move to disengage himself further

    All right?
Valmont Very nice.
Cécile No, I mean, will you go now?

Valmont Oh, I don't think so.
Cécile But you promised.
Valmont I promised to go when you gave me a kiss. You didn't give me
a kiss. I gave you a kiss. Not the same thing at all.

*Silence. Cécile peers at Valmont miserably. He looks back at her, calmly
waiting*

Cécile And if I give you a kiss ...?
Valmont That's what I said.
Cécile You really promise?
Valmont Let's just get ourselves more comfortable, shall we?
Cécile Do you?

*Valmont disposes the cover over them, then leans back to look down on her.
He replaces his hand and Cécile reacts with a start*

Please don't do that.
Valmont I'll take it away. After the kiss.
Cécile Promise?
Valmont Yes, yes.
Cécile Swear?
Valmont I swear. Now put your arms round me.

*Cécile gives a long, surprisingly intense kiss, her eyes tightly closed. Suddenly,
she pulls away from him as much as she can, her eyes now wide with amaze-
ment. Valmont's hand comes slowly up from under the cover. Cécile continues
to look appalled*

See. I told you I'd take my hand away.

SCENE 7

*The following day, 1st October. The low afternoon sun slants in through the
windows of the salon in Mme de Rosemonde's château*

*At first, the room is empty: then Cécile appears, arm-in-arm with Mme de
Merteuil who seems almost to be supporting her. Cécile looks exhausted and
distraught; Merteuil, solicitous*

Merteuil My dear, I really can't help you unless you tell me what's trou-
bling you.
Cécile I can't, I just can't.
Merteuil I thought we'd agreed not to keep any secrets from one another.
Cécile I'm so unhappy.

*Cécile bursts into tears. Merteuil takes her in her arms and soothes her
mechanically, her expression, as long as it's not seen by Cécile, bored and
impatient*

Everything's gone wrong since the day Maman found Danceny's letters.

Merteuil Yes, that was very stupid of you. How could you have let that happen?

Cécile Someone must have told her, she went straight to my bureau and opened the drawer I was keeping them in.

Merteuil Who could have done such a thing?

Cécile It must have been my chambermaid ...

Merteuil Or your confessor perhaps?

Cécile Oh, no, surely not.

Merteuil You can't always trust those people, my dear.

Cécile That's terrible.

Merteuil But today, what is the matter today?

Cécile You'll be angry with me.

Merteuil Are you sure you don't want me to be angry with you?

Cécile looks up at Merteuil, surprised by the acuteness of this idea

Come along.

Cécile I don't know how to speak the words.

Merteuil Perhaps I am beginning to get angry.

Merteuil has spoken quietly; and now there's a long silence. Finally, Cécile takes a deep breath

Cécile Last night ...

Merteuil Yes.

Cécile So that we could exchange letters to and from Danceny without arousing suspicions, I gave Monsieur de Valmont the key to my bedroom ...

Merteuil Yes.

Cécile And last night he used it. I thought he'd just come to bring me a letter. But he hadn't. And by the time I realized what he had come for, it was, well, it was too late to stop him ...

Cécile bursts into tears again; but this time Merteuil doesn't take her in her arms. Instead, she considers her coolly for a moment before speaking

Merteuil You mean to tell me you're upset because Monsieur de Valmont has taught you something you've undoubtedly been dying to learn?

Cécile's tears are cut off and she looks up in shock

Cécile What?

Merteuil And am I to understand that what generally brings a girl to her senses has deprived you of yours?

Cécile I thought you'd be horrified.

Merteuil Tell me: you resisted him, did you?

Cécile Of course I did, as much as I could.

Merteuil But he forced you?

Cécile It wasn't that exactly, but I found it almost impossible to defend myself.

Merteuil Why was that? Did he tie you up?

Cécile No, no, but he has a way of putting things, you just can't think of an answer.
Merteuil Not even no?
Cécile I kept saying no, all the time: but somehow that wasn't what I was doing. And in the end . . .
Merteuil Yes?
Cécile I told him he could come back tonight.

Silence. Cécile seems, once again, trembling on the edge of tears

I'm so ashamed.
Merteuil You'll find the shame is like the pain: you only feel it once.
Cécile And this morning it was terrible. As soon as I saw Maman, I couldn't help it, I burst into tears.
Merteuil I'm surprised you missed the opportunity to bring the whole thing to a rousing climax by confessing all. You wouldn't be worrying about tonight if you'd done that; you'd be packing your bags for the convent.
Cécile What am I going to do?
Merteuil You really want my advice?
Cécile Please.

Merteuil considers a moment

Merteuil Allow Monsieur de Valmont to continue your instruction. Convince your mother you have forgotten Danceny. And raise no objection to the marriage.

Cécile gapes at Merteuil, bewildered

Cécile With Monsieur de Gercourt?
Merteuil When it comes to marriage one man is as good as the next; and even the least accommodating is less trouble than a mother.
Cécile But what about Danceny?
Merteuil He seems patient enough; and once you're married, you should be able to see him without undue difficulty.
Cécile I thought you once said to me, I'm sure you did, one evening at the Opéra, that once I was married, I would have to be faithful to my husband.
Merteuil Your mind must have been wandering, you must have been listening to the opera.
Cécile So, are you saying I'm going to have to do that with three different men?
Merteuil I'm saying, you stupid little girl, that provided you take a few elementary precautions, you can do it, or not, with as many men as you like, as often as you like, in as many different ways as you like. Our sex has few enough advantages, you may as well make the most of those you have. Now here comes your mama, so remember what I've said and, above all, no more snivelling.
Cécile Yes, Madame.

And by now, Mme de Volanges is more or less upon them

She acknowledges Merteuil perfunctorily, but her anxious attention is directed almost entirely towards Cécile, whose expression is now profoundly thoughtful

Volanges How are you feeling now, my dear?

Cécile Oh, much better, thank you, Maman.

Volanges You look so tired. I think you should go to bed.

Cécile No, really, I've . . .

Merteuil I think you should do as your mother suggests. We can arrange for something to be brought to your room. I'm sure it would do you good.

Cécile Well. Perhaps you're right, Madame.

Cécile curtsies to Merteuil and kisses her mother on both cheeks

Volanges I'll come up and see you later on.

Cécile makes a demure exit, watched by the others

When she's left the room, Mme de Volanges turns back to Merteuil

You have such a very good influence on her.

Merteuil I like to think so. But what do you suppose is the matter?

Volanges Didn't she tell you?

Merteuil No, we merely spoke of how she was enjoying the country.

Volanges That makes me even more certain of the cause of her unhappiness. She's pining for that young man. I'm afraid it's beginning to affect her health.

Merteuil Do you think so?

Volanges This morning, I simply asked her how she'd slept, and she threw herself into my arms and cried and cried. (*She sighs deeply. Then she turns decisively to Merteuil*) My dear, I'd be grateful if you would allow me to discuss this with you seriously. I've been brooding about it all day, and now I really feel I need your advice.

Merteuil My dear friend, please, I'd be proud to think I could be of any help to you.

Volanges Well. I've been reconsidering. I really think perhaps I should break off Cécile's engagement with Monsieur le Comte de Gercourt.

Merteuil's head jerks up

He is no doubt a better match than Danceny, but the family, after all, is not decisively superior. Danceny is not rich, of course: but I dare say Cécile is rich enough for both of them. And the most important thing is that they love each other. Don't you agree?

Silence. Merteuil is thinking fast, but the calm in her voice betrays none of this

You think I'm wrong?

Merteuil I have every confidence that your eventual decision will be the right one. If I were able to take a more objective view of the situation, it would only be because, in this case, I am not affected by the altogether praiseworthy emotion of maternal love.

Volanges Please go on, I do rely on your judgement.

Merteuil Well. It seems to me a question of distinguishing what's correct from what's pleasurable. To say this young man is entitled to your daughter just because of his passion for her is a little like saying a thief is entitled to your money. I'm not at all sure how appropriate an emotion love is, particularly within marriage. I believe friendship, trust and mutual respect are infinitely more important.

Volanges And you don't approve of Danceny?

Merteuil There's no denying that, as suitors, there can be no comparison between them. I know money isn't everything: but will sixty thousand a year really be sufficient to maintain the kind of establishment Cécile will be obliged to run, even as Madame Danceny? Of course, I wouldn't dream of suggesting in any way that Danceny has allowed himself to be influenced by financial considerations ...

Volanges But?

Merteuil Precisely.

Silence. Mme de Volanges reflects

But, as I say, this is only an opinion. Naturally, it's your decision.

Volanges Yes.

Merteuil Perhaps you ought not to take it on the strength of a single outburst, which might have any number of, well, medical explanations, for example.

Valmont enters quietly

Volanges Perhaps you're right.

Merteuil In any event, I hope we can discuss it further when we're all back in Paris.

*Merteuil accompanies this remark with a gesture which alerts Mme de Vo-
langes to the fact that Valmont has entered the room. Valmont bows, as the
ladies turn to him*

Valmont Mesdames.

Volanges If you'll excuse me, Monsieur, I must go and make arrangements for some supper to be taken up to my daughter.

Valmont Oh, is she indisposed?

Volanges For the moment.

Valmont The young have such miraculous powers of recuperation. I'm sure she'll soon be back in the saddle. Tell her I hope so, at least.

Volanges Thank you, Monsieur.

Mme de Volanges leaves the room briskly

Valmont watches her go, then turns back to grin at Merteuil

Valmont You see, she can hardly bear to be in the same room with me.

Merteuil But I gather you've had your revenge. Well done.

Valmont So you know?

Merteuil The little one could hardly wait to tell me.

Valmont A favourable report, I trust?

Merteuil On the contrary, Vicomte, if I hadn't spoken to her sharply, I think on your next visit you'd have found her door bolted as well as locked.

Valmont You surprise me. I was malicious enough to use no more strength than could easily be resisted.

Merteuil Still, for some reason she seems to think it was rather an under-hand approach.

Valmont I'd been postponing it, to tell you the truth. But when I heard you were expected today, I wanted to be able to afford you some amusement at least.

Merteuil It's just as well I did decide to look in, because, as it turns out, your initiative came within an ace of sabotaging our whole plan.

Valmont What do you mean?

Merteuil Madame de Volanges was so concerned about Cécile's appearance this morning, she resolved to allow her to marry Danceny after all.

Valmont No.

Merteuil I think I've been able to talk her out of it: but the fact remains, you almost lost us our revenge on Gercourt.

Valmont I could hardly be expected to anticipate this sudden access of compassion. After all, to my knowledge, Mother Volanges has never shown signs of it before.

Merteuil I'm beginning to have my doubts about you, Vicomte. Do you really deserve your reputation? You see, the real reason I consented to spend a night at this lugubrious address was that I was hoping to be shown some tear-stained bit of paper.

Valmont Ah.

Merteuil But I can only assume from what you've been saying that no such document exists.

Valmont No.

Merteuil Probably just as well, no doubt you're exhausted after last night's exertions.

Valmont I think you know me better than that.

Merteuil Well, I wonder. Can you account for this extraordinary dilatoriness?

Valmont Lugubrious or not, I haven't experienced a moment's boredom in all the weeks I've spent here. I appreciate you may have excellent reasons for your impatience, but you mustn't try to deprive me of my simple pleasures. I've explained to you before how much I enjoy watching the battle between love and virtue.

Merteuil What concerns me is that you appear to enjoy watching it more than you used to enjoy winning it.

Valmont All in good time.

Merteuil The century is drawing to its close, Vicomte.

Valmont It's true that she's resisted me for more than two months now; and that's very nearly a record. But I really don't want to hurry things. We go for walks together almost every day: a little further every time down the path that has no turning. She's accepted my love; I've accepted her friendship; we're both aware how little there is to choose between them. Her eyes are closing. Every step she tries to take away from the inevitable conclusion brings her a little nearer to it. Hopes and fears, passion and suspense: even if you were in the theatre, what more could you ask?

Merteuil An audience?

Valmont But you: you're my audience. And when Gercourt is married and Madame de Tourvel eventually collapses, we shall tell everyone, shall we not? And the story will spread much faster than the plot of the latest play; and I've no doubt it will be much better received.

Merteuil I hope you're right, Vicomte, I wish I could share your confidence.

Valmont I'm only sorry our agreement does not relate to the task you set me rather than the task I set myself.

Merteuil I am grateful, of course: but that would have been almost insultingly simple. One does not applaud the tenor for clearing his throat.

Valmont You're right, how could one possibly compare them ... (*He breaks off*)

Mme de Rosemonde enters, followed by Mme de Tourvel

Mme de Rosemonde bustles over to Merteuil to embrace her: Merteuil responds convincingly, but it's clear she has immediately registered the look which passes between Valmont and Mme de Tourvel, a look that indicates that there has indeed been some progress in their relationship

Rosemonde I'm so delighted you could manage to visit us, my dear, even if only for such a short time.

Merteuil I wish I could stay longer, Madame, but my husband's estate ...

Rosemonde Do you know, I was thinking yesterday, it's more than five years since you were last here, with your dear husband. Such a kind and such a vigorous man, who could have imagined ... ah, well ...

Merteuil, who is centrally placed, has been watching Mme de Tourvel and, more particularly, Valmont, who really is lost in contemplation of Mme de Tourvel. She doesn't like what she sees: it clearly troubles her, even though, after only the briefest pause, she manages a civil reply to Mme de Rosemonde

Merteuil Yes, Madame, there's no denying that life is frighteningly unpredictable.

SCENE 8

Two nights later. Valmont's bedroom in the château. It's empty at the moment, a couple of candles casting a dim glow

Presently, Valmont appears, with his dark-lantern, escorting Cécile into the room. They're both wearing dressing-gowns. Cécile looks around the room a trifle apprehensively

Valmont Much the same as your room, you see; but here, you'll be able to make as much noise as you like. (*He's reached the bed and presses down on the mattress*) And the mattress is a little harder.
Cécile Is that good?
Valmont Yes, that's very good.

Cécile gives a whoop, throws off her dressing-gown and jumps on to the bed. She bounces up and down for a moment, then dives in between the sheets. Valmont stands, looking down at her

Cécile Come on.

By way of answer, Valmont stretches out on the bed comfortably, his hands behind his head

Valmont The first thing you must learn is that there is no necessity what-soever for haste. (*He reaches out to caress her*) Now. As with every other science, the first principle is to make sure you call everything by its proper name.
Cécile I don't see why you have to talk at all.
Valmont Without the correct polite vocabulary, how can you indicate what you would like me to do or make me an offer of something I might find agreeable?
Cécile Surely you just say ...
Valmont You see, if I do my work adequately, I would like to think you'll be able to surprise Monsieur de Gercourt on your wedding night.
Cécile Would he be pleased?
Valmont Well, of course, he'll merely assume your mama has done her duty and fully briefed you.

Cécile bursts out laughing

Cécile Maman couldn't possibly talk about anything of the sort.
Valmont I can't think why. She was, after all, at one time, one of the most notorious young women in Paris.
Cécile Maman?
Valmont Certainly. More noted for her enthusiasm than her ability, if I remember rightly, but none the less renowned. There was a famous occasion, oh, before you were born, this would have been, when she went to stay with the Comtesse de Beaulieu, who tactfully gave her a room between your father's and that of a Monsieur de Vressac, who was her acknowledged lover at the time. Yet in spite of these careful arrangements, she contrived to spend the night with a third party.

Cécile laughs again

Cécile I can't believe that; it's just gossip
Valmont No, no, I assure you it's true.
Cécile How do you know?
Valmont This third party was myself.

Cécile's jaw drops. For a moment she statres at Valmont, horrified. He returns a bland smile and, all of a sudden, she can't resist smiling herself. Valmont turns back the covers

Well, we can return to this subject later. During the intervals. You asked me if Monsieur de Gercourt would be pleased with your abilities; and the answer is that even if he isn't, I don't believe it would be difficult to find others who would. Education is never a waste. (*He reaches out and puts a hand round her head, drawing her to him*) Now, I think we might begin with one or two Latin terms.

SCENE 9

Late the following evening. Mme de Tourvel lingers alone in the salon in the château. The card table is out, still scattered with cards

Mme de Tourvel, drifting somewhat aimlessly, glancing at the door from time to time, seems to have no particular reason for being in the room. She starts however and moves briskly to the table to begin tidying away the cards as soon as Valmont, looking elegant but frail, appears in the doorway

Valmont You're alone, Madame.

Valmont advances into the room as Mme de Tourvel answers shakily

Tourvel The others have all decided on an early night. Mademoiselle de Volanges in particular seems to be quite exhausted.
Valmont I must admit to being rather tired myself. (*He arrives at the card table*) May I help you with these? (*He reaches for some cards, brushing her hand in the process, causing her to let go of the cards she's already collected*)
Tourvel No, I'm sure the servants will . . .

Mme de Tourvel moves away from the table in some confusion, heading in the general direction of the chaise-longue. Valmont watches her

Valmont I'm glad to have found you, I very much missed our walk today.
Tourvel Yes . . .
Valmont I fear with the weather as it is, we can look forward to very few more of them.
Tourvel This heavy rain is surely exceptional

Valmont But in a week I shall have concluded my business.

Tourvel I see. (*She stops, affected by this news*)

Valmont begins, very gradually, to move closer

Valmont I may, however, be unable to bring myself to leave.

Mme de Tourvel turns to face Valmont, beset by conflicting emotions

Tourvel Oh, please. You must!

Valmont Are you still so anxious to get rid of me?

Tourvel You know the answer to that; I must rely on your integrity and generosity. I want to be able to be grateful to you.

Valmont Forgive me if I say I don't want your gratitude. Gratitude I can get from strangers; what I want from you is something altogether deeper.

Tourvel I know God is punishing me for my pride. I was so certain nothing like this could ever happen to me.

Valmont Nothing like what?

Tourvel I can't . . .

Valmont Do you mean love? Is love what you mean?

Valmont is beside Mme de Tourvel now and takes her hand. She starts, but does not remove her hand

Tourvel Don't ask me, you promised not to speak of it.

Valmont But I must know. I need this consolation at least.

Silence. Mme de Tourvel still holds Valmont's hand, but cannot bring herself to look at him. Valmont, meanwhile, darts a quick glance at the chaise-longue

Tourvel I can't . . . don't you see? . . . it's impossible . . .

Valmont Of course I understand, I don't want you to say anything, but I must know, I must know if you love me, don't speak, you don't have to speak, I just want you to look at me. Just look. That's all I ask.

Long silence. Then, slowly, Mme de Tourvel raises her eyes to Valmont's

Tourvel Yes.

They're motionless for a moment. Then Valmont releases Mme de Tourvel's hand and raises his arms to embrace her. As he does so, her eyes suddenly go dead and she collapses sideways, obliging him to catch her. She sways in his arms for a moment, then comes to and jerks violently away from him. Then she bursts into tears. She stands for a moment, sobbing wildly, then rushes at Valmont, falls to her knees and throws her arms round his legs

For God's sake, you must leave me, if you don't want to kill me, you must help, it's killing me!

Valmont, somewhat taken aback at first by her intensity, collects himself and lifts Mme de Tourvel to her feet. For a moment they sway together in an ungainly embrace; then Mme de Tourvel's sobs cease abruptly and give way to chattering teeth and almost epileptic convulsions. Startled, Valmont gath-

*ers her up in his arms and carries her over to the chaise-longue where he
deposits her gently. The convulsions continue, her teeth are clenched now, the
blood drained from her face. He leans forward to loosen her bodice as she
stares helplessly up at him. He pauses for a moment, looking down at her, as
her features return to normal. They look at each other. Something passes
between them; and this time it's Valmont who looks away, something almost
like shame darkening his expression. Mme de Tourvel begins to go into shock
again; and Valmont breaks away and runs over to the door, shouting*

Valmont Adèle!

Valmont leaves the room; and a moment later, his voice is heard

(*Off*) Fetch Madame. Madame de Tourvel has been taken ill.

Valmont hurries back into the room and over to the chaise-longue

*As he arrives there, Mme de Tourvel reaches a hand up towards him. He
takes it between both of his. He looks perplexed. He stands in silence,
thoughtful, massaging her hand in his*

*Presently, Mme de Rosemonde appears, shepherded by her Maid. She
clucks anxiously and hurries over towards the chaise longue*

Valmont releases Mme de Tourvel's hand

She seemed to be having difficulty breathing.
Rosemonde Oh, my dear, whatever is it?

Mme de Tourvel stirs, managing a faint smile

Tourvel It's all right, I'm all right now.
Valmont I shall leave her in your capable hands, Aunt. Send Adèle for me
if I can be of any further assistance.

Still looking strangely abashed, Valmont leaves the room

Rosemonde We must send for a doctor, my dear.

Mme de Tourvel is roused from her rapt contemplation of Valmont's departure

Tourvel No, no please, I don't need a doctor, I'm perfectly all right now.
Rosemonde We mustn't take any chances.
Tourvel No, I just ... I must talk to you for a moment.

*Mme de Rosemonde frowns, but without surprise. She turns to gesture at the
Maid*

The Maid curtsies and leaves

Mme de Tourvel motions Mme de Rosemonde to approach

Tourvel Come and sit by me. I can't speak very loud. What I have to say
is too difficult.

Mme de Rosemonde perches on the edge of the chaise-longue looking down at her. Mme de Tourvel takes her hands

I have to leave this house first thing in the morning. I'm most desperately in love.

Mme de Rosemonde, still unsurprised, bows her head

To leave here is the last thing in the world I want to do: but I'd rather die than have to live with the guilt. I don't mind if I die: to live without him is going to be no life at all. But that's what I have to do. Can you understand what I'm saying?

Rosemonde Of course. My dear girl. None of this is any surprise to me. The only thing which might surprise one is how little the world changes. Of course you must leave if you feel it's the right thing to do.

Tourvel And what should I do then? What's your advice?

Rosemonde If I remember rightly, in such matters all advice is useless. You can't speak to the patient in the grip of a fever. We must talk again when you're closer to recovery.

Tourvel I've never been so unhappy.

Rosemonde I'm sorry to say this: but those who are most worthy of love are never made happy by it. You're too young to have understood that.

Tourvel But why, why should that be?

Rosemonde Do you still think men love the way we do? No. Men enjoy the happiness they feel; we can only enjoy the happiness we give. They're not capable of devoting themselves exclusively to one person. So to hope to be made happy by love is a certain cause of grief. I'm devoted to my nephew, but what is true of most men is doubly so of him.

Tourvel And yet . . . he could have . . . just now. He took pity on me, I saw it happen, I saw his decision not to take advantage of me.

Rosemonde If he has released you, my dear child, it's because your example over these last few weeks has genuinely affected and improved him. If he's let you go, you must go.

Tourvel I will. I will.

Mme de Tourvel starts crying again and twists round, letting her head drop into Mme de Rosemonde's lap. Mme de Rosemonde sits, looking down, stroking Mme de Tourvel's hair

Rosemonde There. And even if you had given way, my dear girl, God knows how hard you've struggled against it. There now. (*She strokes Mme de Tourvel's hair*)

The Lights fade to Black-out

INTERVAL

ACT II

SCENE 1

Late October. The principal salon in le Vicomte de Valmont's Paris house

Valmont sits at his desk, writing. He signs with a flourish and looks up as Azolan appears in the doorway and hurries into the room, pausing only to bow deeply

Valmont Well, what treasures do you have in store for me today?

Azolan hands Valmont two letters, one sealed and one unsealed

Azolan A letter to Madame your aunt, sir. And this one, which Julie managed to get to before it was sealed up, to Madame's confessor.

Valmont Ah, very good! (*He runs an eye quickly over the contents of the letter, then proceeds to seal it and his own letter as he speaks*) This is excellent. I have a letter for Father Anselme myself; you may deliver them both when you leave.

Azolan Yes, sir. (*He takes the letters from Valmont*)

Valmont And what news?

Azolan No visitors: there still hasn't been a single visitor since she got back from the country. Kept to her room. Bit of soup last night, but didn't touch the pheasant. Afterwards a cup of tea. Nothing else to report. Oh, yes, there is. You wanted to know what she was reading. She has two books by her bed.

Valmont I don't suppose you found out what they were?

Azolan Course I did, sir, what do you take me for? Let me think, now. One was *Christian Thoughts*, volume two. And the other was a novel written by some Englishman. *Clarissa*.

Valmont Ah.

Azolan See, I was right, wasn't I, sir, there was no need for me to join her staff, now was there? I can find out everything you want to know, no trouble at all.

Valmont I just thought you might prefer to be paid two salaries. As at the time of the Duchesse.

Azolan Oh, well, sir, with Madame the Duchesse, that was quite different, I didn't mind that at all. But I couldn't wear a magistrate's livery, could I, sir, now be fair, not after being in your service.

Azolan indicates his magnificent chasseur's uniform. Valmont smiles, shaking his head. Then Valmont opens a drawer and hands Azolan a small bag of money

Thank you, sir, thank you very much. One day I'll start saving a bit, like you recommended, but I do like to do justice to you.

Valmont After letting Madame de Tourvel leave my aunt's house without even managing to warn me, you're lucky to be working for anybody.

Azolan Now we've been through all that, sir, haven't we? Not even Julie knew she was going till she went.

Valmont How is Julie?

Azolan Seems a bit keener than she was in the country.

Valmont And yourself?

Azolan shakes his head gloomily

Azolan Talk about devotion to duty.

Valmont smiles and looks up as a Footman shows Mme de Merteuil and Danceny into the room

Valmont rises to greet them, dismissing Azolan as he does so, speaking out of the corner of his mouth

Valmont Off you go. Keep it up.

Azolan bows and leaves, together with the Footman

Madame. My dear boy.

Danceny embraces Valmont impulsively

Danceny Thank you, Monsieur, for everything.

Valmont holds Danceny for a moment, smiling wickedly at Merteuil over Danceny's shoulder

Valmont I was afraid I'd been a sad disappointment to you.

Danceny Of course I'm disappointed not to have seen Cécile for more than a month, but I believe I have you to thank for keeping our love alive.

Valmont Oh, as to love, she thinks of little else.

Danceny I had so hoped you'd be able to arrange a meeting between us in the country.

Valmont Well, so had I, I made all the necessary arrangements, but she was adamant.

Danceny I know, she said in her last letter you'd been trying hard to persuade her.

Valmont I did what I could. In many respects I've found her very open to persuasion, but not, alas, on this issue.

Danceny Yes, she said I couldn't do more myself than you've been doing on my behalf.

Valmont She's a most generous girl.

Merteuil What else did she say?

Danceny She said she'd seen signs of a change of heart in her mother. Perhaps in the end she'll come round to the idea of our marriage.

Merteuil That would be wonderful.

Danceny Anyway, how is she, that's what I've really come round to ask you, Monsieur.

Valmont Blooming. I really think the country air has done her good, I think she's even begun to fill out a little.

Danceny Really?

Valmont And of course she sends you all her love. She and her mother will be returning to Paris in about a fortnight, by which time the situation should be resolved one way or the other; and either way, she's longing to see you.

Danceny I don't know how I can bear to go another two weeks without seeing her.

Merteuil We shall have to do our very best to provide some distraction for you.

Danceny Without your friendship and encouragement, I can't think what would have become of me.

Merteuil My dear, if you'd be so kind as to wait in the carriage for a few minutes, there's a matter I must discuss with the Vicomte in private.

Danceny Of course. (*He bows to Valmont and pumps his hand heartily*) I don't know how I can ever repay you.

Valmont Don't give it another thought, it's been delightful.

Danceny smiles charmingly at them both and leaves the room

As soon as he's gone, Valmont and Merteuil burst out laughing and fall into each other's arms. They embrace for a moment and then pull apart, still smiling

Poor boy. He's quite harmless.

Merteuil Well, I must say, I thought Cécile's letter sounded unusually witty.

Valmont So I should hope; I dictated it.

Merteuil Ah, Vicomte, I do adore you.

Valmont I have a piece of news I hope you might find entertaining: I have reason to believe the next head of the house of Gercourt might be a Valmont.

Merteuil What do you mean?

Valmont Cécile is two weeks late.

Merteuil is startled by this: she frowns, assessing its implications

Aren't you pleased?

Merteuil I'm not sure. You have rather overstepped your brief.

Valmont Providing they hold the wedding before the end of the year, I don't see what harm can come of it.

Merteuil No, you're right, the situation does have possibilities. It just makes everything a good deal more chancy. You've used no precautions, then?

Valmont I've tried to give her a thorough grounding in all aspects of our subject: but in this one area, I'm afraid I may have misled her to some extent.

Merteuil shakes her head, amused but still dubious

Your aim was to revenge yourself on Gercourt: I've provided him with a wife trained by me to perform quite naturally services you would hesitate to request from a professional. And very likely pregnant as well. What more do you want?

Merteuil All right, Vicomte, I agree, you've more than done your duty. Shame you let the other one slip through your fingers. I can only assume that's what happened?

Valmont's expression darkens

Valmont I let her go. Can you imagine? I took pity on her. She was ready, the die was cast and the bill was paid. And I relented. And, what do you know, she vanished, like a thief in the night.

Merteuil Why did you let her escape?

Valmont I was ... moved.

Merteuil Oh, well, then, no wonder you bungled it.

Valmont I had no idea she was capable of being so devious.

Merteuil Poor woman, what else could you expect? To surrender and not be taken, it would try the patience of a saint.

Valmont It won't happen again.

Merteuil What you mean is, you won't get the chance again.

Valmont Oh, yes, this time I have a foolproof plan.

Merteuil What, another one?

Valmont Absolutely guaranteed. I have an appointment to visit her at her house on Thursday. And this time, I shall be merciless. I'm going to punish her.

Merteuil I'm pleased to hear it.

Valmont Why do you suppose we only feel compelled to chase the ones who run away?

Merteuil Immaturity?

Valmont I shan't have a moment's peace until it's over, you know. I love her, I hate her, I'm furious with her, my life's a misery; I've got to have her so that I can pass all these feelings on to her and be rid of them.

Merteuil is beginning to look displeased. There's a pause, during which Valmont notices this and does his best to break the mood

Now tell me what's happening in your life.

Merteuil Belleroche is about to fall by the wayside.

Valmont But this is excellent.

Merteuil I have smothered him with so much affection, the poor man can hardly stand up. He's desperately trying to devise some graceful exit.

Valmont Long overdue, in my opinion.

Merteuil And his successor has already been marked out.

Valmont Oh? Who's the lucky man?

Silence. Merteuil considers

Merteuil I'm not sure I care to tell you just at the moment.

Valmont Oh, well, in that case, I shall have to conceal from you the details of my foolproof plan.

Merteuil That seems an acceptable enough bargain.

Valmont frowns, puzzled

Valmont What's the matter?

Merteuil Nothing. I think I may have kept our young friend waiting long enough.

Valmont I shall call on you sometime soon after Thursday.

Merteuil Only if you succeed, Vicomte. I'm not sure I could face another catalogue of incompetence.

Valmont Oh, I shall succeed.

Merteuil I hope so. Once upon a time you were a man to be reckoned with.

Valmont makes to embrace her, but she limits herself to delivering a frosty peck on the cheek and hurries away

Valmont watches Merteuil go, troubled

SCENE 2

Six o'clock in the evening, a couple of days later. The salon in Mme de Tourvel's house, furnished in sombre good taste

Mme de Tourvel sits in an armchair, staring blankly at a piece of embroidery. On the other side of the room is an ottoman

Presently, Valmont is shown in by a Footman; as they appear, Mme de Tourvel makes an effort to stand, but is obliged to sit down again almost immediately. She's trembling. The Footman waits for a moment and is surprised to be dismissed impatiently with a gesture from Mme de Tourvel. Valmont, meanwhile, has bowed deep and now crosses the room to hand Mme de Tourvel a packet of letters, which she takes from him apprehensively. As she inspects them, Valmont, still silent, looks round the room. His eye falls briefly on the ottoman, rests there for a moment and then returns to Mme de Tourvel, who is now looking up at him expectantly

Valmont I understand Father Anselme has explained to you the reasons for my visit.

Tourvel Yes. He said you wished to be reconciled with me before beginning instruction with him.

Valmont That's right.

Tourvel But I see no need for formal reconciliation, Monsieur.

Valmont No? When I have, as you said, insulted you; and when you have treated me with unqualified contempt.

Tourvel Contempt? What do you mean?

Valmont You run away from my aunt's house in the middle of the night; you refuse to answer or even receive my letters: and all this after I had shown a restraint of which I think we are both aware. I would call that, at the very least, contempt.

Tourvel I'm sure you understand me better than you pretend, Monsieur; it seemed to me by far the most . . .

Valmont Forgive me, I didn't come here to trade reproaches. You know your virtue has made as deep an impression on my soul as has your beauty on my heart. I suppose I imagined that made me worthy of you. What has happened is probably a just punishment for my presumption.

Silence

My life has had no value since you refused to make it beautiful: all I wanted from this meeting, Madame, was your forgiveness for the wrongs you think I've done you, so I can at least end my days in some peace of mind.

Tourvel But you won't understand, I couldn't do what you wanted, my duty wouldn't allow me to ... (*Her voice tails off*)

Valmont moves a little closer and begins again

Valmont It was me you ran away from, wasn't it?
Tourvel I had to leave.
Valmont And do you have to keep away from me?
Tourvel I do.
Valmont For ever?
Tourvel I must.

Silence. Then Valmont changes tack again, moving away this time

Valmont Well. I think you'll find your wish that we be separated will succeed beyond your wildest dreams.
Tourvel Your decision is ...
Valmont It's a function of my despair. I'm as unhappy as you could ever have wanted me to be.
Tourvel I've only ever wanted your happiness.

Valmont moves swiftly to Mme de Tourvel, falls to his knees and buries his face in her lap

Valmont How can I be happy without you?

Cautiously, without answering, as if plunging it into boiling water, Mme de Tourvel allows her hand to rest for a few seconds on Valmont's head. Then, as she removes it, he looks up at her fiercely

I must have you or die.

Mme de Tourvel scrambles to her feet and retreats across the room. Valmont watches her and then mutters a bitter aside, loud enough, however, to be heard by her

Death it is.

Silence. Mme de Tourvel is plainly distraught. Valmont appears to make a great effort to calm himself. He rises to his feet

I'm sorry. I wanted to live for your happiness and I destroyed it. Now I want to give you back your peace of mind and I destroy that too. I'm not used to passion, I can't deal with it. At least, this is the last time. So be calm.

Tourvel It's difficult when you are in this state, Monsieur.

Valmont Yes; well, don't worry, it won't last very long.

Valmont picks up the packet of letters, which Mme de Tourvel has let drop by her chair

These are the only things which might weaken my courage: these deceitful pledges of your friendship. They were all that reconciled me to life.

Valmont puts them down on the chair. Mme de Tourvel moves towards him, concerned

Tourvel I understood you wanted to return them to me. And that you now approved of the choice my duty has compelled me to make.

Valmont Yes. And your choice has determined mine.

Tourvel Which is what?

Valmont The only choice capable of putting an end to my suffering

Tourvel What do you mean?

Mme de Tourvel's voice is full of fear. Valmont is beside her now and she doesn't resist as he takes her in his arms

Valmont Listen. I love you. You've no idea how much. Remember I've made far more difficult sacrifices than the one I'm about to make. Now goodbye.

Valmont pulls away from Mme de Tourvel, but she clutches at his wrist

Tourvel No.

Valmont Let me go.

Tourvel You must listen to me!

Valmont I have to go.

Tourvel No!

Mme de Tourvel collapses into Valmont's arms. He begins to kiss her and she responds: for a moment, they kiss each other greedily. Then he sweeps her up in his arms, carries her across the room, sets her down gently on the ottoman and kneels alongside her. She bursts into tears and clutches on to him as if she's drowning. He looks down at her as she sobs helplessly and speaks with unusual tenderness

Valmont Why should you be so upset by the idea of making me happy?

Gradually, Mme de Tourvel stops crying and looks up at him

Tourvel Yes. You're right. I can't live either unless I make you happy. So I promise. No more refusals and no more regrets.

Mme de Tourvel kisses Valmont. He begins, slowly, to undress her

CURTAIN

SCENE 3

The following evening. Merteuil's salon

Merteuil looks up as Valmont burst ebulliently into the room, outpacing the Major-domo

Valmont Success.
Merteuil At last.
Valmont But worth waiting for.

Merteuil flashes a chilly look at him, but he's too exhilarated to notice

Merteuil So it worked, your foolproof plan?
Valmont Of course it wasn't foolproof, I was exaggerating to cheer myself up, but I did prepare the ground as carefully as I could. And I must say, considering these last few weeks my letters were all returned unopened, or rather my letter, since I simply placed it every other day in a fresh envelope, the result has been a genuine triumph. *(By this time, he's taken a seat and he pauses, beaming complacently at Merteuil)*
Merteuil And the plan?
Valmont I discovered, by intercepting her correspondence in the usual way, that she had very wisely decided to change her confidante and was pouring out all her inmost thoughts to my aunt. So very subtly, and aided by the fact I looked terminally exhausted as a result of my exertions with Cécile, I began to hint to my aunt that I was losing the will to live, knowing that this would be passed on. At the same time, I began corresponding with her confessor, an amiably dim-witted Cistercian, whom I more or less forced to arrange the meeting with her, in return for the privilege of being allowed to save my soul, a privilege he will now, poor man, be obliged to forgo. So, the threat of suicide, the promise of reform.
Merteuil I'm afraid I can't say I find that very original.
Valmont Effective though.
Merteuil Tell me about it.
Valmont Well, I arrived about six ...
Merteuil Yes, I think you may omit the details of the seducton, they're never very enlivening: just describe the event itself.
Valmont It was ... unprecedented.
Merteuil Really?
Valmont It had a kind of charm I don't think I've ever experienced before. Once she'd surrendered, she behaved with perfect candour. Total mutual delirium: which for the first time ever with me outlasted the pleasure itself. She was astonishing. So much so that I ended by falling on my knees and pledging her eternal love. And do you know, at the time, and for several hours afterwards, I actually meant it!
Merteuil I see.
Valmont It's extraordinary, isn't it?
Merteuil Is it? It sounds to me perfectly commonplace.

Valmont No, no, I assure you. But of course the best thing about it is that I am now in a position to be able to claim my reward.

Silence. Merteuil considers Valmont coldly for a moment

Merteuil You mean to say you persuaded her to write you a letter as well, in the course of this awesome encounter?

Valmont No. I didn't necessarily think you were going to be a stickler for formalities.

Merteuil Do you know, Vicomte, even if you had arrived with a letter up your sleeve, I'm not sure I wouldn't have had to declare our arrangement null and void?

Valmont What do you mean?

Merteuil I'm not accustomed to being taken for granted.

Valmont But there's no question of that, my dear. You mustn't misunderstand me. What in another case might be taken for presumption, between us, can surely be accepted as a sign of our friendship and confidence in each other. Can't it?

Merteuil I've no wish to tear you away from the arms of someone so astonishing.

Valmont We've always been frank with one another.

Merteuil And, as a matter of fact, I have also taken a new lover, who, at the moment, is proving more than satisfactory.

Valmont Oh? And who is that?

Merteuil I am not in the mood for confidences this evening. Don't let me keep you.

Silence. For a moment, Valmont is at a loss. Then he decides to persevere

Valmont You can't seriously imagine there's a woman in the world I could ever prefer to you?

Merteuil I'm sure you're quite willing to accept me as an addition to your harem.

Valmont No, no, you've misinterpreted. What you think is vanity, taking you for granted: it's really only eagerness.

Merteuil's expression softens slightly, for the first time. Valmont is quick to sense this and immediately tries to press home his advantage

I'd sacrifice anything or anybody to you, you know that.

Merteuil All right, Vicomte, let's try to discuss this calmly, shall we, like friends?

Valmont By all means.

Merteuil There's a strange thing about pleasure, haven't you noticed? It's the only thing that brings the sexes together; and yet it's not sufficient in itself to form the basis of a relationship. You see, unless there's some element of love involved, pleasure must lead directly to disgust.

Valmont I'm not sure I agree with that.

Merteuil Now, fortunately, it's only necessary for this love to exist on one side. The partner who feels it is naturally the happier; while the partner who doesn't is to some extent compensated by the pleasures of deceit.

Valmont I don't think I see your point.

Merteuil My point, Vicomte, is that you and I can in no way conform to this essential pattern, and we may as well admit it. Cardsharps sit at separate tables.

Valmont Yes, and then they compare notes.

Merteuil Maybe: but without, I think, dealing a new hand.

Valmont I can't entirely accept the analogy.

Merteuil Don't worry: I shan't go back on our agreement. I have to go away for a couple of weeks . . .

Valmont What for?

Merteuil A private matter.

Valmont There was a time you kept no secrets from me.

Merteuil Don't you want me to finish what I was saying?

Valmont Of course, I'm sorry.

Merteuil When I've returned, and on receipt of this famous letter, you and I will spend a single night together. I'm sure we shall find it quite sufficient. We shall enjoy it enough to regret that it's to be our last; but then we shall remember that regret is an essential component of happiness. And part the best of friends.

Valmont I think we should take it one step at a time, don't you?

Merteuil No. I think we should be under no illusions.

Valmont You see, I don't think I've ever been unfaithful to you.

Merteuil You know, Vicomte, instead of trying to work on me in this, let's be frank, mechanical fashion, you should be thanking me.

Valmont What for?

Merteuil My courage. My stout resistance. My clear-sightedness. I understand, you see, what's going on.

Valmont Well, that's more than I can claim.

Merteuil I know. You may genuinely be unaware of this. But I can see quite plainly that you're in love with this woman.

Valmont No. You're wrong. Not at all.

Merteuil Have you forgotten what it's like to make a woman happy; and to be made happy yourself?

Valmont I . . . of course not.

Merteuil We loved each other once, didn't we? I think it was love. And you made me very happy.

Valmont And I could again. We just untied the knot, it was never broken. It was nothing but a temporary . . . failure of the imagination.

Merteuil No, no. There would have to be sacrifices you couldn't make and I wouldn't deserve.

Valmont But I told you: any sacrifice you ask.

Merteuil Illusions, of course, are by their nature sweet.

Valmont I have no illusions. I lost them on my travels. Now I want to come home. As for this present infatuation, it won't last. But, for the moment, it's beyond my control.

Silence. Merteuil looks at Valmont for a moment, considering

Merteuil You'll be the first to know when I return.

Valmont Make it soon. I want it to be very soon.

Valmont kisses Merteuil. She seems on the point of submitting to a long kiss, but then she breaks away abruptly and speaks with her usual control

Merteuil Goodbye.

Valmont bows and hurries from the room

Merteuil stands a moment, collecting herself, then she crosses the room and opens a door

He's gone.

Presently, Danceny steps into the room. He embraces Merteuil impulsively and, once again, she submits only briefly

Danceny I thought he'd be here all night. Time has no logic when I'm not with you: an hour is like a century.

Merteuil We shall get on a good deal better if you make a concerted effort not to sound like the latest novel.

Danceny blushes

Danceny I'm sorry, I . . .

Merteuil softens and reaches a hand to Danceny's cheek

Merteuil Never mind. Take me upstairs.

Arm in arm, Merteuil and Danceny begin to move towards the door

SCENE 4

A fortnight later. Afternoon. The salon in Valmont's house

Valmont is pouring another glass of champagne for Émilie, when his Footman enters the room and murmurs something in his ear, which evidently gives him an unpleasant surprise. He controls himself quickly however, gives some instructions and, as the Footman hurries out, turns to Émilie

Valmont Drink up.
Émilie What is it?
Valmont Someone who might well not appreciate your presence here.
Émilie You mean a woman.
Valmont A lady, we might even say.
Émilie Oh, well, then. (*She tosses back her champagne and rises to her feet; then, a thought strikes her*) Not the one you wrote that letter to?
Valmont The very one.
Émilie I enjoyed that.
Valmont And you proved a most talented desk.
Émilie I'd love to see what she looks like.

Valmont Well, you can't.

Valmont moves over to Émilie as she makes a face of mock disappointment, ready to hustle her out of the room. As he reaches her, however, he seems to hesitate a moment, considering

On second thoughts, I don't see why you shouldn't.
Émilie Oo.
Valmont As long as there's no bad behaviour.
Émilie Never unless required.

Valmont looks at Émilie thoughtfully

Valmont Where's your Dutchman?
Émilie Safe in Holland, far as I know.
Valmont And do you have an appointment for tonight?
Émilie Few friends for dinner.
Valmont And after dinner?
Émilie Nothing firm.

Valmont crosses to his desk, opens a drawer and takes out, as before, a small bag of money

Valmont Then perhaps I shall call round on you later. (*He moves over to her and hands her the money*)

> *The Footman is showing in Mme de Tourvel, who stops on the threshold, startled by what she sees*

Émilie I'll be there.

> *Émilie leaves the room, staring with undisguised fascination at Mme de Tourvel, who looks back at her, miserably confused*

Valmont is hovering, torn between his desire to greet Mme de Tourvel and his curiosity to see what will happen

> *It seems as if nothing will; but at the last minute, as she's passing Mme de Tourvel, Émilie is suddenly convulsed with mirth and leaves the room helplessly shaking with laughter*

Mme de Tourvel watches her, horrified; and Valmont, concerned now, hurries over to her

Valmont This is an unexpected pleasure.
Tourvel Evidently.
Valmont Take no notice of Émilie; she's notoriously eccentric.
Tourvel I know that woman.
Valmont Are you sure? I'd be surprised.
Tourvel She's been pointed out to me at the Opéra.
Valmont Ah, well, yes, she is striking.
Tourvel She's a courtesan.

Silence

Isn't she?

Valmont I suppose in a manner of speaking ...

But Mme de Tourvel suddenly turns away, her eyes full of tears, and makes to hurry out of the room. Valmont catches her arm

Tourvel Let me go.
Valmont But what's got into you?
Tourvel I'm sorry I've disturbed you.
Valmont Of course you haven't disturbed me, I'm overjoyed to see you.
Tourvel Please let me go now.
Valmont No, no, I can't, this is absurd.
Tourvel Let go!

Mme de Tourvel wrenches free and Valmont has to cut her off bodily as she makes a determined effort to leave. By now, she's sobbing blindly

Valmont No, wait, wait a minute, it never occurred to me you'd assume, you must let me explain ...
Tourvel No!
Valmont Let's sit down calmly ...
Tourvel And you will never be received at my house again!
Valmont Now.

Valmont's pinioning Mme de Tourvel in his arms. She struggles violently for a moment and then goes limp. He helps her across to a sofa and sits them both down, keeping an arm round her

Now listen.
Tourvel I don't want your lies and excuses!
Valmont Just listen to me. Just hear me out, that's all I ask, then you can judge.
Tourvel I don't want to.
Valmont Have a glass of champagne ...
Tourvel No!

But for some reason, though still trembling, Mme de Tourvel quietens down and watches Valmont, transfixed, as he speaks with unruffled calm

Valmont Unfortunately, I cannot unlive the years I lived before I met you; and, as I've explained to you before, during those years, I had a wide acquaintance, the majority of whom were no doubt undesirable in one respect or another. Now it may surprise you to know that Émilie, in common with many others of her profession and character, is kind-hearted enough to take an interest in those less fortunate than herself. She has, in short, the free time and the inclination to do a great deal of charity work: donations to hospitals, soup for the poor, protection for animals, anything which touches her sentimental heart. From time to time, I make small contributions to her purse. That's all.
Tourvel Is that true?
Valmont My relations with Émilie have for some years now been quite blameless. She's even done a little secretarial work for me on occasion.

Since I now know your feelings on the matter, I shall of course take steps to make sure she is never received here again.

Tourvel Why did she laugh?

Valmont I've no idea. Malice perhaps? Jealousy? Girls of that class are often unpredictable. I'm at a loss to explain it.

Tourvel Well, does she know about me?

Valmont No doubt she made what, in view of my past, must be accepted as a fair assumption.

Silence. Mme de Tourvel looks at Valmont, almost convinced

Tourvel I want to believe you.

Valmont I knew you were coming up, you were announced. Do you seriously imagine, if I'd felt the slightest guilt about Émilie, I would have allowed you to see her here?

Tourvel I suppose not.

Valmont No.

Tourvel I'm sorry.

Valmont No, no, no, it's I who must apologize. It was most insensitive of me. Some relics of my old persona remain. That was the thoughtless action of a man who had never met you.

Mme de Tourvel begins to weep again, but softly this time, relieved. She buries her face in Valmont's chest. He watches her for a moment, his expression profoundly contented

I didn't think it was possible for me to love you more, but your jealousy . . .

Valmont breaks off; and now he too seems genuinely moved. Presently, Mme de Tourvel looks up at him.

Tourvel I love you so much.

Valmont continues to look at Tourvel, disarmed by her sincerity, suddenly no longer in command of his emotions, his expression pained and uncharacteristically tender

SCENE 5

Ten days later. Evening. Mme de Merteuil's salon. A domestic tableau

Danceny lies on the sofa with his head in Merteuil's lap. She plays idly with his hair. After a time, at first unseen by the others and unaccompanied by servants, Valmont appears in the doorway. He assesses the scene and then clears his throat, causing Danceny to shoot upwards in confusion. Merteuil looks at Valmont, her eyes cold

Valmont Your porter appears to be under the impression that you are still out of town.

Merteuil I have in fact only just returned.

Valmont Without attracting the attention of your porter? I think it may be time to review your domestic arrangements.

Merteuil I'm exhausted from the journey. Naturally I instructed my porter to inform casual callers that I was out.

Valmont seems to check a retort at this point, and turns instead, smiling, to Danceny

Valmont And you here, as well, my dear young friend. The porter would appear to be having a somewhat erratic evening.

Danceny Oh, well, I, erm, yes.

Valmont I'm glad to find you, I've been trying to contact you for some days.

Danceny Have you?

Valmont Mademoiselle Cécile returns to Paris after an absence of over two months. What do you suppose is uppermost in her mind? Answer, of course, the longed-for reunion with her beloved Chevalier.

Merteuil Vicomte, this is no time to make mischief.

Valmont Nothing could be further from my mind, Madame.

Danceny Go on.

Valmont Imagine her distress and alarm when her loved one is apparently nowhere to be found. I've had to do more improvising than an Italian actor.

Danceny But how is she? Is she all right?

Valmont Oh, yes. Well, no, to be quite frank with you. I'm sorry to tell you she's been ill.

Danceny springs to his feet, horrified

Danceny Ill!

Valmont Whether it was brought on by her anxieties it's impossible to say, but it seems about a week ago they were compelled to send for the surgeon in the middle of the night, and for a while he was very concerned.

Danceny But this is terrible!

Valmont Calm yourself, my friend, she has been declared well on the road to recovery and she is convalescing now. But you can well imagine how desperate I've been to find you.

Danceny Of course, my God, how could I have not been here at such a time? How can I ever forgive myself?

Valmont chooses not to answer this: he looks at Merteuil for a moment, assessing the damage

Valmont But look, I hate to be the bearer of bad tidings. All is well now with Cécile, I assure you, I have it from the surgeon himself. And I shan't disturb you further. (*He produces a piece of paper from an inside pocket*) It's just that I had a letter, the contents of which I thought might be of interest to the Marquise.

Silence. The ball is in Merteuil's court and she makes the effort to reach a decision

Merteuil I think perhaps I should spend a few minutes with the Vicomte on a private matter. Why don't you go upstairs, I shan't be long.

Danceny But I'm worried about Cécile.

Merteuil I don't think there's anything to be done at this hour of the evening. You can send to enquire after her tomorrow.

Danceny Well, all right, if you say so.

Merteuil I do.

Danceny I'm sorry, Vicomte, I ...

Valmont Don't upset yourself, dear boy, everything is as it should be.

Danceny Thank you. Thank you.

Danceny leaves the room

Silence. Merteuil is about to speak, when Valmont interrupts her by handing her the letter. Merteuil gives it a cursory glance and then hands it back to Valmont

Merteuil I see she writes as badly as she dresses.

Valmont I think I'm right in saying that in this case it's the content not the style which is the essential. But perhaps there's something else we should discuss first.

Merteuil I do hope you're not going to be difficult about Danceny: it was a complete coincidence he arrived at the gates at the same moment as my carriage.

Valmont Really, my love, this is hardly worthy of you. Given the uncharacteristic mystery you made about the identity of your new lover and Danceny's and your simultaneous disappearance from Paris, I would have to have been a good deal stupider even than you seem to assume I am, not to have reached the obvious conclusion. If Danceny and your carriage arrived at the gates at the same moment, I imagine the main reason was because he was in it.

Merteuil You're quite right, of course.

Valmont And furthermore, I happen to know that this moment of which we speak occurred two days ago.

Merteuil Your spies are efficient.

Valmont So much for my being the first to know when you returned. A lesser man might allow himself to get angry.

Merteuil Such a man might risk losing his ability to charm, without necessarily enhancing his power to persuade.

Silence. Valmont restrains himself and decides to change tack

Valmont I must say I'm not surprised you chose to be reticent about so manifestly unsuitable a lover.

Merteuil My motive had nothing whatever to do with his suitability.

Valmont I mean I know Belleroche was pretty limp, but I think you could have found a livelier replacement than that mawkish schoolboy.

Merteuil Mawkish or not, he's completely devoted to me, and, I suspect, better equipped to provide me with happiness and pleasure than you in your present mood.

Valmont I see.

Slightly winded by this, Valmont lapses into an injured silence. Merteuil's mood, however, now she has regained the initiative, seems to have improved

Merteuil So is it really true the little one has been ill?

Valmont Not so much an illness, more a refurbishment.

Merteuil What can you mean?

Valmont's energy returns at the prospect of telling his story

Valmont Once she'd returned to Paris, some money for the porter and a few flowers for his wife were enough to enable me to resume my nocturnal visits: which, incidentally, don't you agree, shows up Danceny's initiative in a very poor light. However, the ease of it no doubt made us overconfident, and one night last week, as we were resting after our exertions, the door, which we'd forgotten to lock, suddenly blew open. The most dreadful shock. Cécile threw herself out of bed and tried to jam herself between it and the wall. A sudden severe backache gave way to some unmistakable symptoms. After that, it was a real test of ingenuity, getting the surgeon round, without giving ourselves away.

Merteuil But you evidently succeeded?

Valmont Can you imagine, my dear, it turned out Cécile wasn't even aware of being pregnant in the first place. She certainly doesn't devote any undue energy to thinking.

Merteuil Well, Vicomte, I'm sorry about the loss of your son and Gercourt's heir.

Valmont Oh, I thought you'd be pleased, you seemed notably disgruntled about it when I first told you.

Merteuil Once I got used to the idea, I began to enjoy it. I think you should make another attempt, don't you?

Valmont I rather felt the moment had come to pass her on to young Danceny.

Silence. Merteuil considers for a moment

Merteuil No, I'm not sure that would be advisable just now.

Valmont Oh, you don't?

Silence

Merteuil If I thought you would be your old charming self, I might invite you to visit me one evening next week.

Valmont Really.

Merteuil I still love you, you see, in spite of all your faults and my complaints.

Valmont I'm touched. What else will you exact before honouring your obligations?

There's a pause, during which Merteuil looks mischievously at Valmont

Merteuil I have a friend, who became involved, as sometimes happens, with an entirely unsuitable woman. Whenever any of us pointed this out to him, he invariably made the same feeble reply: it's beyond my control, he would say. He was on the verge of becoming a laughing-stock. At which point, another friend of mine, a woman, decided to speak to him seriously, and, most importantly, drew his attention to this linguistic foible, of which he'd previously been unaware, and told him his name was in danger of becoming ludicrously associated with this phrase for the rest of his life. So do you know what he did?

Valmont I feel sure you're about to tell me.

Merteuil He went round to see his mistress and bluntly announced he was leaving her. As you might expect, she protested vociferously. But to everything she said, to every objection she made, he simply replied: it's beyond my control.

Long silence. Eventually, Valmont rises

Valmont I must leave you to your lessons.

Merteuil doesn't answer. She watches Valmont, smiling, as he moves, deep in thought, towards the door

SCENE 6

The following afternoon. The salon in Mme de Tourvel's house

Her Footman shows Valmont in, and Mme de Tourvel springs to her feet, unable to conceal her delight. Valmont however looks strained and weary and advances almost reluctantly into the room, as the Footman leaves them

Mme de Tourvel runs over to Valmont and buries herself in his arms. He embraces her almost involuntarily, bracing himself against what is to come

Tourvel You're only five minutes late, but I get so frightened. I become convinced I'm never going to see you again.

Valmont carefully disentangles himself and puts some distance between them before he speaks

Valmont My angel.

Tourvel Is it like that for you?

Valmont Oh, yes. At the moment, for example, I'm quite convinced I'm never going to see you again.

Silence. Mme de Tourvel frowns, trying to make sense of this

Tourvel What?

Valmont I'm so bored, you see. It's beyond my control.

Tourvel What do you mean?

Valmont After all, it's been four months. So, what I say. It's beyond my control.

Tourvel Do you mean ... do you mean you don't love me any more?

Valmont My love had great difficulty outlasting your virtue. It's beyond my control.

Tourvel It's that woman, isn't it?

Valmont You're quite right, I have been deceiving you with Émilie. Among others. It's beyond my control.

Tourvel Why are you doing this?

Valmont Perhaps your merciless vulnerability has driven me to it. Anyway, it's beyond my control.

Tourvel I can't believe this is happening.

Valmont There's a woman. Not Émilie, another woman. A woman I adore. And I'm afraid she's insisting I give you up. It's beyond my control.

Suddenly, Mme de Tourvel rushes at Valmont, fists flailing. They grapple silently and grimly for a moment, before she screams at him

Tourvel Liar!

Valmont You're right, I am a liar. It's like your fidelity, a fact of life, no more nor less irritating. Certainly, it's beyond my control.

Tourvel Stop it, don't keep saying that!

Valmont Sorry. It's beyond my control.

Mme de Tourvel screams

Why don't you take another lover?

Mme de Tourvel bursts into tears, shaking her head and moaning incoherently

Just as you like, of course. It's beyond my control.

Tourvel Do you want to kill me?

Valmont strides over to Mme de Tourvel, takes her by the hair and jerks her head up, shocking her into a moment's silence

Valmont Listen. Listen to me. You've given me great pleasure. But I just can't bring myself to regret leaving you. It's the way of the world. Quite beyond my control.

When Valmont lets go of her hair, Mme de Tourvel collapses full-length, moaning and sobbing helplessly. Valmont crosses to the doorway and turns to look back at her. His triumphant expression has lasted only a moment; and now gives way to a queasy, haunted, tormented look. His eyes are full of fear and regret. For a moment, it's almost as if he's going to run back to help her. Abruptly Valmont turns and guiltily scuttles away

SCENE 7

About a week later. A December evening in Mme de Merteuil's salon

Merteuil sits at a small escritoire, writing

After a time Valmont appears in the doorway, once again unannounced. Merteuil, with her back to the door, doesn't see him, but as he approaches, she looks up, hearing a footstep, and speaks without turning round

Merteuil Is that you? You're early.
Valmont Am I?

Merteuil spins around, startled; to be greeted with an ironic bow from Valmont

I wanted to ask you: that story you told me, how did it end?
Merteuil I'm not sure I know what you mean.
Valmont Well, once this friend of yours had taken the advice of his lady-friend, did she take him back?
Merteuil Am I to understand ...?
Valmont The day after our last meeting, I broke with Madame de Tourvel. On the grounds that it was beyond my control.

A slow smile of great satisfaction spreads across Merteuil's face

Merteuil You didn't!
Valmont I certainly did.
Merteuil Seriously?
Valmont On my honour.
Merteuil But how wonderful of you. I never thought you'd do it.
Valmont It seemed pointless to delay.
Merteuil With the anticipated results?
Valmont She was prostrate when I left. I called back the following day.
Merteuil You went back?
Valmont Yes, but she declined to receive me.
Merteuil You don't say.
Valmont Subsequent enquiries I made established that she had withdrawn to a convent.
Merteuil Indeed.
Valmont And she's still there. A very fitting conclusion, really. It's as if she'd been widowed. (*He reflects for a moment, then turns to Merteuil, radiating confidence*) You kept telling me my reputation was in danger, but I think this may well turn out to be my most famous exploit. I believe it sets a new standard. I think I could confidently offer it as a challenge to any potential rival for my position. Only one thing could possibly bring me greater glory.
Merteuil What's that?
Valmont To win her back.
Merteuil You think you could?
Valmont I don't see why not.

Merteuil I'll tell you why not: because when one woman strikes at the heart of another, she seldom misses; and the wound is invariably fatal.
Valmont Is that so?
Merteuil I'm so convinced it's so, I'm prepared to offer any odds you care to suggest against your success.

Some of the self-satisfaction has ebbed out of Valmont's expression

You see, I'm also inclined to see this as one of my greatest triumphs.
Valmont There's nothing a woman enjoys as much as a victory over another woman.
Merteuil Except, you see, Vicomte, my victory wasn't over her.
Valmont Of course it was, what do you mean?
Merteuil It was over you.

Long silence. The fear returns to Valmont's eyes. He begins to look concerned. Merteuil, on the other hand, has never seemed more serene

That's what's so amusing. That's what's so genuinely delicious.
Valmont You don't know what you're talking about.
Merteuil You loved that woman, Vicomte. What's more you still do. Quite desperately. If you hadn't been so ashamed of it, how could you possibly have treated her so viciously? You couldn't bear even the vague possibility of being laughed at. And this has proved something I've always suspected. That vanity and happiness are incompatible.

Valmont is very shaken. He's forced to make a great effort, before he can resume, his voice a touch ragged with strain

Valmont Whatever may or may not be the truth of these philosophical speculations, the fact is it's now your turn to make a sacrifice.
Merteuil Is that right?
Valmont Danceny must go.
Merteuil Where?
Valmont I've been more than patient about this little whim of yours, but enough is enough and I really must insist you call a halt to it.

Silence

Merteuil One of the reasons I never remarried, despite a quite bewildering range of offers, was the determination never again to be ordered around. I decided if I felt like telling a lie, I'd rather do it for fun than because I had no alternative. So I must ask you to adopt a less marital tone of voice.
Valmont She's ill, you know. I've made her ill. For your sake. So the least you can do is get rid of that colourless youth.
Merteuil I should have thought you'd have had enough of bullying women for the time being.

Valmont's face hardens

Valmont Right. I see I shall have to make myself very plain. I've come to spend the night. I shall not take at all kindly to being turned away.

Merteuil briefly consults the clock on her desk

Merteuil I am sorry. I'm afraid I've made other arrangements.

A grim satisfaction begins to enliven Valmont's features

Valmont Ah. I knew there was something. Something I had to tell you. What with one thing and another, it had slipped my mind.

Merteuil What?

Valmont Danceny isn't coming. Not tonight.

Merteuil What do you mean? How do you know?

Valmont I know because I've arranged for him to spend the night with Cécile. (*He smiles charmingly at Marteuil*) Now I come to think of it, he did mention he was expected here. But when I put it to him that he really would have to make a choice, I must say he didn't hesitate for a second. I'd dictated a letter for Cécile to send him, as insurance, but as it turned out, there wasn't any need to be so cautious. He knew his mind.

Merteuil And now I know yours.

Valmont He's coming to see you tomorrow to explain and to offer you, do I have this right, yes, I think so, his eternal friendship. As you said, he's completely devoted to you.

Merteuil That's enough, Vicomte.

Valmont You're absolutely right. Shall we go up?

Merteuil Shall we what?

Valmont Go up. Unless you prefer, this, if memory serves, rather purgatorial sofa.

Merteuil I believe it's time you were going.

Silence

Valmont No. I don't think so. We made an arrangement. I really don't think I can allow myself to be taken advantage of a moment longer.

Merteuil Remember I'm better at this than you are.

Valmont Perhaps. But it's always the best swimmers who drown. Now. Yes or no? Up to you, of course. I wouldn't dream of trying to influence you. I therefore confine myself to remarking that a no will be regarded as a declaration of war. So. One single word is all that's required.

Merteuil All right. (*She looks at Valmont evenly for a moment, almost long enough for him to conclude that she has made her answer. But she hasn't. It follows now, calm and authoritative*) War.

Black-out

SCENE 8

Dawn on a misty December morning in the Bois de Vincennes

On one side of the stage, Valmont and Azolan: on the other, Danceny and a Manservant. Valmont is making his selection from a case of épées, held open for him by Azolan. He weighs now one and now the other in his hand. Danceny, meanwhile, waits impatiently, in shirt-sleeves, épée in hand, shifting from one foot to the other. Finally, as Valmont seems to be on the point of making his decision, Danceny can restrain himself no further

Danceny I know it was easy for you to make a fool of me when I trusted you, but out here I think you'll find there's very little room for trickery!

Danceny's Manservant looks at him disapprovingly, but Valmont responds calmly to this breach of etiquette

Valmont I recommend you conserve your energy for the business in hand.

Valmont makes his final choice of épée and lays it on the ground while Azolan helps him off with his coat and on with a black glove. Then, Valmont and Danceny approach one another and take up the en-garde position. At a sign from Azolan, the duel begins, fierce and determined, Valmont's skill against Danceny's aggression. For some time, they're evenly matched, with Valmont, if anything, looking the more dangerous. Then Danceny succeeds, more by luck than good judgement, in wounding Valmont in whichever is not his sword arm

A short pause ensues and then, after a murmured consultation between Valmont and Azolan, the duellists resume the en-garde position and begin again. This time it's Danceny who looks to have the initiative. For some reason, connected or not with his wound, Valmont seems to have lost heart, or even interest, and at one point when the deflection of a too-committed attack by Danceny seems to leave him wide open, Valmont fails to take advantage of what looks like a golden opportunity

Eventually, it's some piece of inattention very close to carelessness on Valmont's part which allows Danceny through his guard with a thrust which enters Valmont's body somewhere just below his heart. There's a moment of mutual shock, and then Danceny withdraws his sword and Valmont staggers a couple of steps towards him, before subsiding with a slight gasp to the ground. Azolan hurries to him, falls to one knee and lifts Valmont's head

I'm cold.

Azolan runs to get Valmont's coat, as Danceny turns to his Manservant

Danceny Fetch the surgeon.
Valmont No, no.
Danceny Do as I say.

The Manservant hurries away as Azolan manages to drape Valmont's coat around him

Danceny stands alone, uneasy, some way off, so that Valmont has to make the considerable effort to raise his voice above a murmur, to be sure that Danceny will hear him

Valmont A moment of your time.

Danceny reluctantly approaches. Valmont begins to try to struggle up on one elbow, and Azolan drops to one knee to support him

Two things: a word of advice, which of course you may ignore, but it is honestly intended; and a request. (*He pauses, a little breathless*)

Danceny Go on.

Valmont The advice is: be careful of the Marquise de Merteuil.

Danceny You must permit me to treat with scepticism anything you have to say about her.

Valmont Nevertheless, I must tell you: in this affair, both of us are her creatures.

Danceny looks at Valmont thoughtfully, not answering for a moment

Danceny And the request?

Valmont I want you to get somehow to see Madame de Tourvel...

Danceny I understand she's very ill.

Valmont That's why this is most important to me. I want you to tell her I can't explain why I broke with her as I did, but that since then, my life has been worth nothing. I pushed the blade in deeper than you just have, my boy, and I want you to help me withdraw it. Tell her it's lucky for her that I've gone and I'm glad not to have to live without her. Tell her her love was the only real happiness I've ever known.

Danceny I will.

Valmont Thank you.

The silence is broken by snatches of birdsong. Danceny, suddenly overcome, puts a hand up to brush away a tear. Azolan, watching, lets his indignation show

Azolan It's all very well doing that now.

Valmont Let him be. He had good cause. It's something I don't believe anyone's ever been able to say about me. (*He raises a hand towards Danceny: but the effort of doing so is too great, and he slumps back before Danceny can take his hand. He's dead*)

SCENE 9

New Year's Eve. Once again, three ladies at cards in the salon of Mme de Merteuil's hôtel. This time, it's Merteuil herself, Mme de Volanges and Mme de Rosemonde, the latter in mourning

For a while, the play proceeds in silence, until it comes to Mme de Rose-monde's turn and she is looking away, lost in thought, no longer concentrating on the game. Merteuil discreetly clears her throat, to no effect. Finally Mme de Volanges leans forward and touches Mme de Rosemonde's elbow

Volanges Madame.

Mme de Rosemonde comes to with a start

Rosemonde Forgive me. At my age, it seems reasonable to hope to be spared any further personal tragedies. But two in the space of a few days ...

Merteuil Of course, Madame.

Volanges And I was just thinking: when you were last in Paris, a year ago, do you remember that conversation we had? We were trying to decide who was the happiest and most enviable person we knew; and we both agreed it was Madame de Tourvel.

Merteuil You were with her, were you not, when she died?

Volanges I was with her from the day after she ran away to the convent. I shall never forget those terrible sights. When she kept ripping away the bandages after they bled her. The delirium and the convulsions. How she wasted away.

Merteuil listens, her practised expressionlessness intact, except for the glitter of satisfaction in her eyes. Mme de Volanges shakes her head, sighs, resumes

All the same, I think she might have recovered if that unfortunate young man hadn't somehow managed to let her know your nephew was dead. After that, she simply lost the will to live. Apparently, as he was dying, the Vicomte managed to convince Danceny that Madame de Tourvel was the only woman he'd ever loved.

Merteuil That's enough!

All of them, even Merteuil herself, are startled by the sharpness of this involuntary remark. Merteuil hastens to paper over the crack, by adding a quiet explanation to Mme de Volanges

I think we should respect the sensibilities of our friend.

Rosemonde Oh, no, I firmly believe that was the truth.

Merteuil Well, perhaps, I can't see how we shall ever know ... (*Her voice is uncharacteristically shaky. She makes an effort to regain her usual self-control and changes the subject*) And your daughter?

Volanges She seems quite adamant. I've appealed to her and pleaded with her but she won't budge. I did want to ask your advice about this, both of you. Monsieur de Gercourt is expected back any day now. Is there nothing to be done? Must I really break off such an advantageous match?

Merteuil Oh, surely not.

Rosemonde I'm afraid you must.

Volanges But why?

Rosemonde I'd rather you didn't ask.

Merteuil I think you must provide a reason, Madame, if you ask our friend to sacrifice so glorious a future. (*Her fighting spirit has returned now, and her voice is as crisp and decisive as ever*)

Volanges To be honest with you, Madame, and in spite of his crime, I'd rather marry Cécile to Danceny than see my only child become a nun.

Rosemonde As a matter of fact, I've heard from Danceny. He sent me a very strange letter. From Malta.

Volanges Oh, that's where he's run away to?

A silence falls, Merteuil is busy digesting what Mme de Rosemonde has said. When she's done so, she turns to Mme de Volanges

Merteuil On second thoughts, my dear, I suppose it might be best to defer to Madame's wisdom and experience. Perhaps you should leave Cécile in the convent.

Volanges But there must be a reason?

Silence. No one seems disposed to add anything and Mme de Volanges's question hangs in the air. Eventually, Merteuil speaks, with all her customary authority

Merteuil This has been a terrible few weeks. But time passes so quickly. A new year tomorrow and more than half-way through the eighties already. I used to be afraid of growing old, but now I trust in God and accept. I dare say we would not be wrong to look forward to whatever the nineties may bring. Meanwhile, I suggest our best course is to continue with the game.

Merteuil's words seem to exert a calming effect on her companions: and indeed, they resume playing. The atmosphere is serene

Very slowly, the Lights fade; but just before they vanish, there appears on the back wall, fleeting but sharp, the unmistakable silhouette of the guillotine

FURNITURE AND PROPERTY LIST

Only essential properties etc. are listed here. Further dressing is at the director's discretion

ACT I

SCENE 1 Merteuil's salon

Set: Opulent furniture includes:
Chairs
Card table
Sofa
Escritoire
Screen
Bell pull
Playing cards

SCENE 2 Rosemonde's salon

Set: Furniture includes:
Various chairs
Armchair
Chaise-longue
Card table
Tapestry frame; *on it* tapestry and threaded needle

SCENE 3 Émilie's bedroom

Set: Furniture includes:
Bed
Bureau; *in it:* pen, inkwell, writing paper

SCENE 4 Merteuil's salon

Set: As Scene 1

SCENE 5 Rosemonde's salon

Set: As Scene 2, plus playing cards, shawls, book

Personal: **Valmont:** Letter, key

SCENE 6 Cécile's bedroom

Set: Bed
Bell pull

Off stage: Dark lantern (**Valmont**)

SCENE 7 Rosemonde's salon

Set: As Scene 2

SCENE 8 Valmont's bedroom

Set: Furniture includes:
                Bed
                Lighted candles

Off stage: Dark lantern (**Valmont**)

SCENE 9 Rosemonde's salon

Set: As Scene 2, plus playing cards on card table

ACT II

SCENE 1 Valmont's salon

Set: Furniture includes:
                Sofa
                Desk; *on it:* paper, pen, inkwell
                In Drawer: small bag of money
                Table

Off stage: Two letters (**Azolan**)

SCENE 2 Tourvel's salon

Set: Furniture, in sombre good taste, includes:
                Armchair
                Ottoman
                Piece of embroidery

Off stage: Letters (**Valmont**)

SCENE 3 Merteuil's salon

Set: As Act I Scene I

SCENE 4 Valmont's salon

Set: As Act II Scene 1, including:
                In desk drawer: small bag of money
                On table: opened bottle of champagne, glasses

SCENE 5 Merteuil's salon

Set: As Act I Scene 1

Personal: **Valmont:** piece of paper

SCENE 6 Merteuil's salon

Set: As Act I Scene 1
                On escritoire: paper, inkwell, pen

SCENE 8 Bois de Vincennes

Set: Case of epées

Personal: **Danceny:** epée
                Azolan: black glove

SCENE 9 Merteuil's salon

Set: As Act I Scene 1

LIGHTING PLOT

Act I, Scene 1

To open: Interior, summer evening
No cues

Act I, Scene 2

To open: Interior, early evening, sun shining through french windows

Cue 1   **Rosemonde** exits   (Page 10)
          Very gradually lower lights as evening falls

Act I, Scene 3

To open: Interior, candlelight

Cue 2   **Valmont:** "We'll finish it later, shall we?"   (Page 15)
          Fade to Black-out

Act I, Scene 4

To open: Interior, autumn afternoon
No cues

Act I, Scene 5

To open: Interior, autumn, early afternoon

Cue 3   **Valmont** settles to read his book   (Page 25)
          Fade lights to those of early evening

Act I, Scene 6

To open: Darkness

Cue 4   **Valmont** enters   (Page 27)
          Bring up lights slightly

Act I, Scene 7

To open: Interior, autumn, afternoon, sunlight through the window
No cues

Act I, Scene 8

To open: Interior, night, candlelight

Cue 5   Valmont enters   (Page 36)
               Bring up lights slightly

Act I, Scene 9

To open: Interior, late evening

Cue 6   Mme de Rosemonde strokes Mme de Tourvel's hair   (Page 40)
               Fade to Black-out

Act II, Scene 1

To open: Interior, autumn

No cues

Act II, Scene 2

To open: Interior, autumn, early evening

No cues

Act II, Scene 3

To open: Interior, autumn, evening

No cues

Act II, Scene 4

To open: Interior, late autumn, afternoon

No cues

Act II, Scene 5

To open: Interior, late autumn, evening

No cues

Act II, Scene 6

To open: Interior, late autumn, afternoon

No cues

Act II, Scene 7

To open: Interior, December, evening

Cue 7   **Merteuil:** "War."   (Page 62)
          Blackout

Act II, Scene 8

To open: Exterior, December, misty morning

No cues

Act II, Scene 9

To open: Interior, December

Cue 8   **Merteuil:** "... to continue with the game."   (Page 66)
          *Very slowly fade lights, before light goes, bring up briefly a silhouette of
          a guillotine on back wall. Fade to Black-out*

EFFECTS PLOT

ACT I

No cues

ACT II

MADE AND PRINTED IN GREAT BRITAIN BY
LATIMER TREND & COMPANY LTD PLYMOUTH
MADE IN ENGLAND